Bruja

by
Morag Higgins

Bruja

Published by
Fisher King Publishing
The Studio
Arthington Lane
Pool-in-Wharfedale
LS21 1JZ
England

ISBN 9781906377-50-2

Cover design by Rick Armstrong
Edited by Mary-Ellen Wyard

Morag Higgins has been riding for over thirty five years and teaching for three decades. She has had the privilege to have known and worked with many, many horses in her career having participated in several disciplines such as jumping, dressage, one-day eventing, showing and western riding.

Traditionally trained, Morag was herself a very traditional trainer and rider producing many horses to top level in a variety of disciplines, but through it all she was always seeking more. She began to study with the Intelligent Horsemanship Association in 1999. After qualification she was made the Recommended Associate for Scotland in 2002 and continued in this role for four years.

In 2005 Morag had the good fortune to ride on a clinic with top American trainer Mark Rashid. A fellow Martial Artist, she instantly understood his ethos and he has been the real inspiration that guided her down the path leading to the development of the Equido Training system. One of the first Natural Horsemanship systems to be recognized as a National Qualification.

Morag trains from her yard, Ross Dhu Equestrian, in Quarter, Larkhall, Scotland and continues to grow and develop as a Natural Horsewoman and Trainer.

Morag and Mark Higgins are the authors of Equido, Horsemanship for the 21st Century.

Respect

WHAT IS YOUR QUESTION? Is it, walk trot or gallop? Ask me in the right way and I can give you all that you wish.

If you demand, then all you will do is contort my body with pain and twist my nature into the ignorance and arrogance held in your own mind.

When asked properly, I would crawl on my knees for you, I'd break my back if you wanted, I would give up my life for you, and all I ask in return is for a warm bed, some food, a kind word and love from every touch from your hand.

To think or whisper the language I know, which is so complex to some people, but so simple for others to understand for they know what can be achieved with kindness and love.

Speak softly the words that I know and I'll give you the key's to heaven, shout and all of hell's demon's will follow you forever or until you learn to listen and ask in the right way.

I am the wind,
I am life's force,
I am a part of you,
And will be forever.

Mark Higgins

For my parents, James and Margaret Colquhoun, without whose support my life would never have taken this journey.

To my husband Mark for his strength and forbearance, his tolerance and patience and most of all for just being the best husband in the world.

And of course to Bruja, my teacher, my guide, my best friend and my baby girl. You allowed me to grow with you; you carried me to many a victory. You were my true inspiration.

May your light continue to burn in the hearts of all who knew you and in those who will come to know you through the pages of this book.

Morag Higgins

Contents

The Parting

Choking pain closed my throat as the phone receiver quietly clicked into place. The blurred vision of my window drew me inwards to my memories, to my life. Today my best friend would die and I would have to do for her what she couldn't do for herself. I would have to take her life and set her free from misery.

Agony swept through me as my very heart beat at my chest, sobs racking my body, my tears washing the morning grime from my face. I couldn't be like this for her. Today of all days I must be strong. I must give her the peace she deserved and ease the break from this world by sending her onwards with love. My husband called quietly from below, "Its Bruja isn't it?" "Yes," I whispered, "It is time for her to go."

He came up and sat beside me, instinctively knowing that I did not need him to hug nor comfort me; he simply sat and let me remember.

The Meeting

I pulled the seed off the plant we knew as the 'hairy man', closed my eyes and spoke from my heart, "I wish, I wish I had a horse." Reverently I planted the seed in the damp soil hoping it would grow and grant my dream. I must have single-handedly planted most of the dandelions in our Glasgow housing scheme in Mount Vernon; each and every one carried my prayer, a prayer that would soon be answered.

For as long as I could remember, all I ever wanted was to ride and own a horse. "That wean is horses daft," was the war cry of my Mum whenever she caught me galloping up and down the back green with her good sweeping brush, one of my Dad's socks (invariably one of his best ones) stuffed with paper to make the shape of a head and tied to the end of the brush shaft.

Of course my Grandfather got the blame of my obsession. While my Dad was at work and my Mum went to her part time job, Gran and Grandad looked after my brother and me. Grandad would sit me on his knee and tell me stories of the big horses that he had looked after and how they used to pull the bread vans in Glasgow. I could almost smell the aroma from the freshly baked bread, as it must have mingled with the scent of the horses. He told me all of their names and the adventures they would get into. One name I still recall was "Chum". One hot summer's day Grandad made the fatal mistake of taking pity on the poor sweating horse and stopped outside a well-known "Tally" shop near Thornliebank. This shop sold the best homemade Italian ice cream in the area and he bought Chum an ice cream. "Tae cool down efter hiking up that big hill," he said. Of course every time he took that particular route with Chum, the horse would stop outside the same shop, summer or winter, refusing to move till my Grandad had bought him an ice cream.

One of my most treasured possessions is a chrome-plated shoe from Chum and it hangs still in my house.

Amid those wonderful stories my imagination was fired; I too longed for that special friendship that I could tell my Grandfather had with all of his horses. On a visit to my Dad's Uncle Charlie, a "doonhaimer" from Dumfriesshire, I remember what Mum said the first time that she met him. They had been talking for a while about things in general and she had mentioned my Grandad and the bread horses. He had cried, "Och lassie, I've followed the horses for years." "Oh" replied my mother, "I didn't know you were a betting man?" Uncle Charlie wheezed with laughter, "No, no lassie, I wis a ploughman, you know the plough horses!" Uncle Charlie was a retired ploughman.

The highlight of that visit was when Uncle Charlie said we could go and see one of his horses, which was retired in a field not far away. Uncle Charlie whistled and I stood glued to the spot, transfixed as I watched as a huge white horse lolloped down the field towards us. I was allowed to pat him, give him slices of bread and given the most honoured privilege of sitting on his back. That was me hooked; I had found heaven on earth and knew, at that tender age, that one way or another, horses would be a part of my life.

My Grandfather died when I was four, but the longing he had placed in my heart grew and grew. I drove my parents to the edge of insanity as I begged and begged my Mum and Dad for a horse. "You're too young", "we can't afford one," were the replies. To a child this seemed the ultimate torture. Even though I was fully aware of our lack of money, my life would be so much less if I had to resign myself to the fact that I would never be able to have a real live horse? A fate worse than death!

When I was eight my friend Scott was allowed to go to our local riding school, Foxley Equestrian Centre, for riding lessons. I begged and cried that I also be allowed to go and eventually my Mum gave in. My first lesson cost the enormous sum of £1.25 and lasted a full hour. It was an hour of pure ecstasy for me. A chance to sit on a real horse and learn the majestic art of horse riding. As I look back I am sure my parents thought that if they allowed me to continue to ride that I would grow out of it, that it would just be the passing fancy of a child.

At the age of twelve I was still riding once a week and was given the opportunity of "looking after" one of my friend's horses at the weekend. My friend kept her horse at her uncle's farm. In return for doing some simple work sweeping and cleaning and generally tidying up around the farm, I was allowed to brush, feed and ride Style, a sixteen point two hands high Grey heavyweight Hunter. I am sure now that Style never realised that anyone was on his back! We were only allowed to ride in one field and my friend and I would jump on the horses without any hat, saddle or bridle and set off round as fast as we could go. I looked after Style, every weekend, rain or shine for a full year. I think by this time my Mum realised that I was not going to get this out my system, that this was something that would not go away.

"OK, you have one week to buy a horse. I only have £500 to spend and if you don't get one this week then I will be buying a new three piece suite." That was the ultimatum I was given when I was 13. Where do you buy a horse? I didn't know. I was not going to let a little lack of knowledge foil me. I was being given a chance to get something that I had wanted all my life and I wouldn't let it slip away. I picked up the telephone directory and looked up "Horses". See "Dealers", was the suggestion, so I looked up "Dealers". The nearest Horse Dealer to us was Billy Stewart in Lesmahagow. So, taking the bull by the horns, I phoned the yard. I think that whoever answered the call must have thought I was just some kid fooling around. "Hello, I want to buy a horse. Do you have any for sale?" "Yes," was the reply. I was stumped, what do I say now? "How much are they?" "How much do you want to spend?" Should I tell him the full price or should I play it cool? At that point my Mum overheard my conversation. Taking the phone from me she apologised to the man and saved the day. After sitting listening to one side of a conversation I was getting more excited by the second. It felt as if my heart was in my mouth. Mum hung up the phone. It was agreed. We would go down to the yard and look at two horses the Dealer felt were suitable for me.

We arrived at the yard at night. My Mum, Dad and Gran, brought along because she knew about horses from Grandad, all squashed into the car. Mr Stewart was there to meet us, along with his Head Lad. He led us into the main stable block. Yet again I was awe struck; it was my first sight of the most wonderful horses in the most magnificent rugs. "Those are Show jumper's hen. I think they are a bit too expensive for you," was the response to my wide-eyed appreciation. "This one here would be good for your daughter," Mr Stewart continued addressing my Mum and Dad. I looked at a pretty little bay pony with big friendly eyes and a cheeky face. I liked him, but he was smaller than I had wanted. "I was looking for something a little bigger, around fifteen point two hands high," I said, trying to sound as knowledgeable as I possibly could. I had read in a book that this was a good average height for horses and I knew that even if I grew a bit taller I would still be able to ride an animal over fifteen hands high.

I expected an argument but there was none. "Oh

right, let's look at this one then." I was led to another stall with a larger Grey horse lurking within. I didn't like the look on his face. Mr Stewart put a protective arm around me to hold me back as he let his lad bring the horse out. "It's all right," I said, "I don't like this one very much. Could I see the bay again please?"

Mr Stewart patiently took us back to the little bay. "This horse is older and more experienced than what you were looking for. I know you wanted a five year old, but I think that this horse will teach your daughter much better. It is a competition horse and ready to do shows." My Mum and Dad nodded, agreeing with Mr Stewart's sound advice. "He is a little bit more expensive though, this one is £800." My Mum and Dad's face fell, as there was no way we could afford that much. It was a disaster. My heart hit my boots. I was going to lose out after all. At that moment I heard a clatter of hooves behind me. Looking round I saw what looked like an enormous black stallion with a white face pawing the ground in frustration. "Is that a stallion?" I asked in awe. "No hen, that's a mare just off the boat frae Ireland. She's only angry because she can't eat her hay quickly with the bit in her mouth. She's just a baby you see, only four, never been ridden and as green as grass." "Can I see her?" I asked. Mr Stewart obliged and opened the stable door. His lad took off the Dumb Jockey that the mare was wearing to help her get her used to the bit and bridle.

The horse immediately moved to the back of the box, her side pressed against the back wall, her head high in fear and confusion. She was almost black with four white socks and a white blaze. I walked straight up to her. "Careful hen, she's just a baby!" said Mr Stewart. I wasn't afraid, I could hear my Grandfather saying to me, "This is your horse, take her." I touched her shoulder and gently patted her. Turning to Mr Stewart I said, "I want this one please." His response was one of concern and worry. "Listen hen, this is just a young horse, she's never been ridden, I don't know what she's like. I can't tell you anything about her. Why don't you look at the other horses again, they can be ridden now." "It's all right, this is the one I want." I looked at my Mum and Dad. It was clear they recognised the determination in my face. "But Morag, listen to what Mr Stewart says, he knows about these things," was the half-hearted response. At that point my Gran spoke up, "If this is the one the wean wants then this is the one she should have." Mr Stewart must have realised he was fighting a losing battle. "How much is this horse?" asked my Dad. "I'll give her to you for £500," replied Mr Stewart, "but here's a suggestion. I don't sell anything from this yard that I don't know about. Leave the horse here for a week. I'll back and break her. I'll school the other two on and then your daughter can ride all three next time then decide which one she wants. If after a month it doesn't work out, I'll take the horse back again. How's that?" And so it was agreed.

That was such a long week. I hardly slept and the minutes seemed to drag by as if some mysterious hand had reached out to slow all time so that seconds appeared as minutes and minutes were stretched into hours. At night I lay awake with the very excitement of seeing my horse again.

A week later we were back at the yard. I only wanted to see the "wee dark mare", but I was given a ride on the Grey first. The horse was obedient and well-schooled, but all I could think about was "the wee dark mare". Finally Mr Stewart let me ride her. She was very, very green. All she could do was walk, trot, and a rather scrappy canter. I could tell that she didn't really have a clue as to what I wanted her to do, but I could sense that she was trying her best. She didn't understand, but she had the courage and kindness to try so very hard to please a total stranger. "I still want this one," I gasped as I pulled her to a stop. It was a done deal.

Mr Stewart must have felt sorry for us; he sold us the horse, saddle, bridle, head collar and delivered her to the livery yard I was going to keep her at, all for just £550. The day she arrived, he led her off the horsebox, handed me the rope and I led her the quarter mile walk down the driveway of the yard.

It was as if we both knew, that horse and I, as we

walked down that dusty track in the late sun of the day that these were the first steps together on a journey through life that was the beginning of a companionship that would last twenty years.

The Arrival

"Very nice little horse," "I like her colour," "What's her name?" were the barrage of questions fired at me by all the other livery clients. I was standing in the schooling area of a local DIY yard surrounded by very knowledgeable, very experienced people. A very green horse and an even greener owner.

I had read a book a long time ago called "The Wild Heart". The horse in the book was called "La Bruja". The story is one of great courage, love, loyalty and sacrifice. It has a rather sad but at the same time uplifting ending and I swore that day as I turned the last page, tears in my eyes and a lump in my throat, that if I ever got the opportunity of owning my own horse, I would call it Bruja.

"Her name is Bruja," I said, my heart completely bursting with pride as I led her to her first real home.

Of course I had never thought about where I would buy straw, hay or feed for my horse and so she arrived on the yard to an empty concrete box. "Take a couple of my bales of straw and hay for tonight. You can give me them back when you get your own," was the kind offer made by Carol, who owned a horse called Ben. With her help we put down the bed and made sure Bruja was comfortable. "She's settled down quickly," said Carol, "eating her hay quite happily." We left Bruja munching and walked about the yard meeting the other horses. Carol talked away about the other animals and how so and so had got cast one day. I looked at her bemused and asked, "What do you mean cast?" "It's when a horse lies down and rolls and gets its legs stuck against a wall and can't get up." "Is that bad?" I asked. "Oh, yes, the horse could panic and give itself colic or injure its legs." "Colic?" Carol's eyes narrowed as she regarded me thoughtfully, "Colic, you know, sick, ill." "Can horses get sick?" This was a complete revelation to me. I never knew that a horse could get sick. All the horses that I had ever ridden were always ready and tacked up for me to ride. I suddenly realised that I may be an adequate rider, but I knew absolutely nothing about looking after horses. Carol was pointedly staring away from me, not answering my question. "Carol, can I ask a big favour?" She looked at me again. "I don't know much about looking after horses. I can ride OK, but now I know how little experience I have when it comes to care, can you teach me how to do it right?" Carol smiled, "I'm so glad you asked me," she said, "I wouldn't have liked to offer; some people may take it the wrong way, but you've got your head screwed on straight." I can honestly say that if it wasn't for Carol teaching me all she knew, I would never have survived the first year.

My parents were very clear as to where the responsibility for looking after my new horse lay. I had recently purchased a paper round and my profit of £10 per week was spent on my stable rent. My Mum and Dad paid for everything else of course, but in those days things were a little cheaper. My Mum and Dad were not really horsy folk and were nervous of Bruja at first. Mr Stewart had suggested that we keep Bruja in her stable for the first week, just till she got to know us and so, every night, my Mum bravely volunteered to lead Bruja round the exercise square as I mucked out her stable. My Mum would keep her eyes shut and kept saying to herself, "I'm walking the dog, I'm walking the dog!" Bruja would quietly plod round behind her as quiet as a lamb.

One night as I came round to ask Mum to bring her in I found them standing in the middle of the yard. "What's wrong?" I asked. "I think there is something wrong with her eyes," was my Mum's concerned response. "I was walking round and we were passing this jump but instead of Bruja walking round it she walked into it!" Bruja was a little bit bigger than my Mum and, probably still thinking she was walking the dog, my Mum had squeezed through a gap that was too small for the horse, which quite sensibly had simply stopped.

Over the years I have often looked back in wonder at my Mum and Dad, but for their help, their kindness patience and understanding I believe I could not have managed. Dad was nervous of horses and had never handled them. In spite of this he would go up to the yard before his early shift, 5.00am, and turn Bruja out into the field. One morning Carol was up early and saw Dad leading Bruja with a strange contraption over her head. Carol burst out laughing when she realised that he had her head collar on upside down. Again it was my fault. I never thought to show him how to put it on. Bruja had patiently been lead out to the field for at least a month with what must have been a rather uncomfortable harness.

I sense that Bruja knew how nervous my Mum and Dad were and she was careful to be quiet and gentle around them. However, Bruja definitely had a rather twisted sense of humour. I remember my Dad waiting for me after going up to the yard early to catch Bruja and bring her in. He looked rather annoyed and very hot. "That crazy horse of yours has just dragged me the length of the field." "What do you mean?" I asked. "I went out to catch her, but every time I got close to her she walked away. I just kept walking after her, and she led me up the entire field, all twenty acres to the top corner then stopped and let me catch her!" One of Bruja's favourite jokes no doubt.

I knew enough to know that a horse that is to be worked must be shod properly. I asked Carol who her Farrier was and she told me, "Mr Jim Jarvie".

I phoned Mr Jarvie and asked if he would come out and shoe Bruja. "How old is the horse?" asked Mr Jarvie. "Four," I replied. "Has she ever been shod before?" "No," I said. There was a pause and then, "OK, what size are her feet?" I was silent for a moment, "She's fifteen point two so whatever size they normally take," was my chanced guess. Mr Jarvie sighed but patiently replied, "Take a ruler or measuring tape and measure toe to heel and across the widest part of her foot for all of her feet then call me back." Feeling like a twit I promised I would call him back the next night.

That evening I tried to measure Bruja's feet. I had always been used to horses that were trained and so I didn't realise that a horse had to be shown how to pick up its foot. When I grabbed her leg and pulled it up Bruja must have got one hell of a fright. She immediately pulled her leg away. "What's wrong with her Carol, she won't let me pick up her feet?" "Does she know how?" asked Carol. "What do you mean?" "Has she been taught?" continued Carol as she made her way down to my box. "Let me see what she does," she suggested. I picked up her leg and again Bruja stamped it down, this time a bit more firmly. "OK," said Carol, "she just doesn't understand. She thinks you're trying to trip her up. Do it again slowly and when she tries to pull away say no and hold on as long as you can." Ladies and gentlemen the pantomime was about to begin.

I struggled to hold Bruja's leg up long enough for Carol to get a quick measure of her foot before it came crashing down. "I think you had better work with her before Mr Jarvie comes out," suggested Carol.

I called Mr Jarvie and gave him the shoe sizes. I didn't mention about Bruja not knowing how to pick up her feet. I had two days before Mr Jarvie was due to visit and I thought that was plenty of time to teach her, oh how naive I was!

As promised, Mr Jarvie appeared on Saturday and came into Bruja's stall. She was snorting and huffing at the strange mixture of horse and iron smells on his clothes. He quietly ran a hand down her neck. "Well old thing, let's have a look at your feet." He expertly picked up her leg, taking Bruja completely by surprise and studied her feet. As time ticked by, all of two seconds, Bruja decided she had stood long enough and pulled away. "Now then, now then old thing, just you stand up." I was truly impressed as Mr Jarvie refused to let go of her leg even as she tried to hop away on the other three. Finally he put her foot down and moved to her back leg. I am ashamed to say that I still wasn't able to hold her leg up for any length of time and she went through the routine of cow-kicking and flicking out with her leg as Mr Jarvie gamely hung on. He put her foot down and turned round to me. "OK, you will need to work with her a bit longer. I'll come back in a fortnight and shoe her then. Every night you do what I did and refuse to let go, no matter what she does." I nodded and promised I would work with her.

I was as good as my word and despite being kicked about a stable, not maliciously I must add, I stuck it out for the full two weeks. I was bruised and battered but I didn't blame Bruja. She didn't understand why she must stand on three legs and have her hoof hit with a hoof pick. By the time Mr Jarvie returned she would stand quietly holding up each front leg when requested. Her back legs were a different story. It was always a race against the clock before she would try to pull away. The attempts she made were becoming less determined, but it was an effort to hold on all the same.

Everything was going fine as Mr Jarvie worked. He was very quiet and very patient, letting her put her foot down frequently to rest. Bruja repaid his kindness by not giving him any hassle, even as he nailed the shoes onto her feet. Finally he came to the last leg, her back left. She let him trim the foot, she let him prepare the shoe and tap in each of the nails. She let him start to snip off the sharp ends of the nails as they stuck out of her foot and just as he was finishing the last one and I was feeling immensely relieved she let him have it.

A quick cow-kick and stamp down, the sharp nail

slashed Mr Jarvie's leg as it snapped past, tearing his trousers and drawing blood. "Bruja!" I shouted, "Stand up straight!" my hand slapping her belly with a resounding smack. To his credit and somewhat unbelievably, Mr Jarvie never said a word. He quietly picked up her foot and snipped the end off of the nail. "She's just getting tired and fed up," he said, "I'll tidy up the feet and finish off." That was the first time Mr Jarvie shod Bruja. He never on any occasion raised his voice to her and for her part she never kicked him again.

Mr Jarvie shod Bruja roughly once every six weeks for the next twenty years. Although he never said it he must have spotted me for the greenhorn I was and after a while realised I was thirsty for knowledge.

With immense patience he explained all of the inner workings of the horse's leg and foot. How to treat minor ailments, how to spot lameness, how to shoe to correct faults and how to remove a shoe and trim a foot. Over the years I relied on Mr Jarvie's expert knowledge, knowledge that he has always been ready to impart. If ever Bruja went lame I knew a call to Mr Jarvie would soon bring him here to examine her legs and to proffer advice and assistance. There are Farriers nowadays that are only in the game for the money. Mr Jarvie is not one of those, yes, he works to make a living, but it's more than that, he shoes horses because he cares about the animals he helps.

Getting To Know One Another

In those first few months I learned an awful lot about looking after horses. But I also learned a lot about people. One thing that astounded me was that everyone had his or her own ideas and methods. I realised very quickly that some people who thought they were "experienced" would, without any prompting, gladly stand and lecture you about how they would do this or that and how so-and-so doesn't have a clue and does it all wrong. Time after the time I found the really knowledgeable people tended not to push advice onto you but gave simple answers if questioned and perhaps coaxed. The horsy world I'm afraid appears to have more than its fair share of unpleasant people, a lot of whom think they know more simply because they have more. Sometimes the characters in the novels of Jilly Cooper really do reflect real life more than fiction

Then there was Carol and how very glad I was that she was kind enough to take me under her wing. I still had to do everything myself and she would only bail me out if I had been struggling away without gaining any ground.

"Everyone," she would say, "has his or her own ways. Some are good, some are bad. The trick is to listen and watch them all, and then use those methods that seem to work for you and your horse." Grandad had often told me, "If ye want to know the real nature of someone then look at their horse." This piece of wisdom has stayed with me all of my life and I have to say it is the truth. A nasty, twisted person will usually have a nasty, twisted horse. A good, honest and kind person will likewise have a good, honest and kind horse. Could it be that the animals simply mirror their owners?

Carol owned with her sister a gentle, quiet little thoroughbred with a wicked sense of humour. Finally I mentioned to Carol in passing my thoughts about the connection between people and their horses. She laughed and said, "Of course it's true. Horses can hear what people think and tend to copy and mimic their owners. It is possible to take a bitter and twisted animal and with the right owner transform it into a kind and loving beast. You have to know what you're doing of course and it does take time." I never forgot what Carol said and always held it in the back of my mind. When in years to come I was faced with an apparently "dangerous" animal, I would look first at the owner.

Poor Bruja I'm afraid had quite a rude awakening to the world of the working horse. I was used to riding schooled horses and had been told from the very beginning that the best way to train a horse is to ride it as though it were a trained horse. Unfortunately, most of the horses I had ridden up until then had been Riding School Veterans who, bored with the constant monotony, would think up all kinds of ways for dodging work. The only way to deal with them was to let them know who was boss right from the beginning. The moment they first refused to do anything we were told to hit them with the stick and make them do as they were told. The only good thing about my riding training was that I could recognise all manners of evasions and pig headedness in horses. Sadly at that time I couldn't recognise confusion and misunderstanding.

It never occurred to me for a moment that Bruja might not have understood exactly what I wanted. So, if I asked her to do something and she hesitated or refused, she would be punished. Bruja would then do anything in the hope that it was the right thing. In this trial and error fashion Bruja learned that when kicked with both legs she had to go faster. When her head was pulled to the right or left she had to turn and when both reins were pulled she had to stop. In a way I was doing the right thing, but with the light of wisdom I now see that poor Bruja must have had a confusing start to her education and I realise through this how yet again she demonstrated how truly kind and generous was her nature.

I was taught that everything for a horse must be black or white, right or wrong. They must understand from the very beginning that if they don't do as they are told they will be punished. With Bruja the punishment was quickly reduced to a warning, "Right, ENOUGH!". She knew that should my warning go unheeded then a sharp smack with the stick or hand would follow. As a result Bruja's manners with people were impeccable. Everyone who met her commented on how quiet and gentle she was; anyone who really knew her understood that her real nature was much more fiery and dominant.

I learned later in life that in the wild, older mares are in charge of the herd. It is up to them to discipline youngsters and teach them how to behave in horse society. If a youngster is out of line then the boss mare will give them a sharp nip or "punch" with her teeth. If this is not heeded then a warning kick will be given. If the youngster is really badly behaved then they will be isolated from the herd and left out on their own, put into Coventry so to speak. A horse can kick and bite far harder than any human, so it is imperative that the horse is never the boss. If that happens then you will find them disciplining the owner and unfortunately they just might accidentally injure or kill with a reprimanding kick. However, I always knew that Bruja had the brains and temperament to be a Boss Mare, in other words, if she were left in the wild with a herd, she would be the most dominant and aggressive mare and so the herd leader. Right from the start I had to make it clear that I was Boss Mare and she could either be my friend or subordinate. Her quiet and gentle nature was the result of a happy and secure horse that knew the boundary lines of good behaviour very clearly. She was quite aware of what would happen should those boundaries be overstepped and I was there to witness it. She also knew that she had a strong Boss Mare as her friend. This was highlighted on more than one occasion when at shows, if we were standing around with a group of riders dismounted and talking, she would pick a fight with a neighbouring horse then quickly hide behind me if the outraged neighbour retaliated. Sometimes having a horse trust you completely isn't always safe!

After the first month of looking after Bruja my Mum suggested that I let my cousin Susan come up and spend some time at the stable. Susan was as daft about horses as me. I went to dancing classes on a Saturday morning so it was suggested that Susan could go up and look after Bruja while I was dancing. I remember the first time Susan came up to the yard. It was on a Sunday and I was to show her how to look after Bruja. I was a bit concerned about the whole affair. I had wanted a horse for so long that I wasn't really sure about sharing her with anyone. No one else at the yard shared their horse, why should I? When Susan arrived she was obviously nervous about my reaction. She understood exactly how I must have felt. She had begged for a horse for as long as she could remember and knew the mixed feelings I must have been having. To my surprise, as soon as I saw her nervousness I realised how stupid I was being.

That first day Susan was up was the best laugh I had ever had. It was great to be able to talk to someone about Bruja, what she did, what she wouldn't do, how pretty she was and so on. Most people who own their own horse simply can't be bothered to listen to all of the silly little things that someone else's horse does. Susan was the first person I had met that truly understood how I felt.

Our friendship was born. Susan would regularly come up at weekends. On Saturdays she would ride Bruja alone, then on Sundays we would share the work. I looked after Bruja myself through the week, but I must admit that I so looked forward to the weekend when the three of us were together.

The Adventures Begin

For Bruja the first years in her new home were both exciting and eventful. She made a lot of mistakes, got more than her fair share of injuries and achieved so much in such a short space of time all the more wondrous considering the handicap she had of an idiot for an owner.

The second time Bruja was due to be shod was also the first time she went out on the roads by herself. Up until then Bruja had only been ridden in the exercise yard or along the private road. She was still green and struggling to understand the complexities of being ridden. One of the other girls, Ann suggested that I get Bruja used to traffic by coming with her and her horse, Beau, down a private lane and onto the main road to watch the cars go by. The main road was the dual carriageway that runs past Glasgow Zoo. At that time it was the only access road to the M74 South and so was extremely busy with cars, buses, lorries and all manner of traffic. I thought that this was a great idea. Once or twice a week, it always seemed to be at night and pitch black, we would ride down the road, without reflective gear I may add, that hadn't been invented yet for horses. Bruja would stand calmly transfixed by all the noise and the lights flashing past her, completely at ease and unconcerned.

The Saturday that she was due to be shod was a wet drizzly day and the field was thick with mud. I went out to catch her to bring her in to dry in plenty of time for Mr Jarvie arriving.

The horses were sheltering behind the stable block at a gate that was never used by the livery owners, only by the yard owner for her horse. Next to the gate was a kennel for the yard owner's pet goat. The goat, being smart, was sleeping in its kennel out of sight. I didn't fancy struggling through the mud to catch Bruja and so I decided to sneak her out through the forbidden gate. I had her caught and out of the gate with it securely locked behind me and almost in the clear when disaster struck. The goat, being curious about the noise, popped out of its kennel just as we were passing. Bruja, who had never seen a goat before, took off across the gravel yard dragging me behind on the end of the lead rope. I hung on gamely for a few strides, but eventually let go as I toppled face first to the ground.

Bruja, with her head up looking behind her at the goat, continued her mad dash for freedom. To my horror she didn't look where she was going and crashed into the back of the yard owner's parked car. Her head came swinging downwards as her chest rammed into the boot of the car, shattering the rear windscreen with her teeth. With a grunt of surprise she pulled her head out of the rear seat, gave herself a shake and trotted over to meet me as I hobbled, open mouthed and horrified at the damage, little bits of gravel pebble dashing my face. I was relieved to see that she appeared none the worse for her car wrecking and quickly put her in her stable. I knocked on the yard owner's door with great trepidation. "I'm afraid there's been a bit of an accident," I said as the woman answered the door. Without any further explanation I looked at their car. "What on earth happened?!" she shouted. "Bruja ran into your car," I mumbled. "Don't worry, she's insured and we will pay for the damage." This seemed to calm the woman down a bit, but I could tell she was pretty angry.

I knew Bruja was insured, but I didn't know any of the details, so, tacking her up I decided to ride down to my house in Mount Vernon which was three miles away in a housing scheme and report the accident to my parents before Mr Jarvie arrived. I rode Bruja down the now familiar private road and out onto the dual carriageway.

Fortunately for me there was a wide pavement to ride along and I trotted this totally amazed if not dazed horse at a furious pace. I guess it was lucky that I was so angry with her and that with her usual sensitivity she knew it. I dread to think how she would have behaved in other circumstances. All the riding school horses I had ridden out were completely bomb proof in traffic and so it didn't occur to me at all that Bruja might be afraid of bus shelters, road signs, grit bins, signs painted on the road and all the other paraphernalia that we take for granted and to which we do not give a second glance.   As we approached each new item and she hesitated I gave her a sharp smack and told her to "get on".   So single-minded was I to get home that she sensed my determination and despite what for her must have been a strange and terrifying experience she bravely carried on. When the rider trusts the horse, the horse will nearly always trust the rider.

The only time I gave her a moment to look was when we had to squeeze through a really narrow gap between a bus shelter and stone wall. I had to duck and rely on Bruja walking through calmly. By this time I had begun to realise just how unsure she must be and consented to give her a pat of reassurance when she successfully squeezed through the gap.

That first time out on a main road Bruja negotiated traffic lights, housing schemes with its dogs, children, lawn mowers, cars, sounds and smells On the main road she saw for the first time and up close lorries and buses as they hurtled past at forty to fifty miles an hour only a few feet from her. Imagine my Mum and Dad's surprise when I rode Bruja up our garden path and into the back garden. Letting her munch the lawn as a reward I dived into the house to tell them about the accident. "Why didn't you just phone us from the yard?" my Dad asked. I stared at him dumbfounded. It had never occurred to me to ask the yard owner if I could use their phone. Leaping back onto Bruja I set off again back to the yard to meet Mr. Jarvie. Once more Bruja trotted happily along what must have been strange roads, more confident now that she had seen more things in a night than a lot of horses see in a lifetime.

Yet again, as I look back, I am amazed at how obedient and well-behaved Bruja was. To have travelled along that kind of road at four years of age and completely alone took a lot of courage on her part. It also highlights the love and trust that she had for me. It never occurred to her to question what I was asking and she relied on me to keep her out of danger. If the rider is confident and unafraid then the horse will do just about anything. My confidence was born out of ignorance and while I would dearly like to believe that this just goes to prove that fortune favours the brave, I think it also favours the foolhardy.

Learning Together

As I relied on my parents for transport to and from the yard I was quite often left to my own devices for several hours at a time.

For any young person who is dreaming of owning their own horse they should be prepared to work hard. From Monday to Friday from 4.00pm to 6.00pm I did my paper round. I would then have a quick bite to eat before being taken back to the yard at 6.30pm. By the time I returned home it would be 9.30pm and between then and 10.30pm I would do my homework. At the weekend I joined Susan on Saturday afternoons from 12.00pm until 6.00pm and all day Sunday from 9.00am to 5.00pm.

The time spent at the yard was not all hard work. Susan and I liked to play games with Bruja. If she were standing munching her hay we would attempt to sneak into the stable block. Crouching low we would creep up to her stable without her noticing. If we made it to her door, we would watch her through the gaps in the wooden board and almost imperceptibly whisper her name. We always tried to time our whisper with the munching of the hay. If she caught the slightest sound she would stop chewing and motionless, listen intently. Trying desperately not to laugh we would whisper her name again, very quietly and continue to do this until she finally caught us out. If we were heard she would run to the door and stare down at us, blowing on our heads as pleased as punch that she had found us.

Bruja's stable was the first in a row of five indoor boxes lined up against one wall. The corridor leading out of the block was wide enough for one horse, but too narrow in which to turn a horse around. Halfway along the corridor were the remains of an old blocked off doorway and it was just possible to squeeze a horse around at that point only.

One of our favourite games was "chases". We would shut the door to the outside, close all the stable doors except for Bruja's and the last box. The walls dividing the stables were not full height, probably four feet at most. We would stand in the top box and call out to Bruja, encouraging her to come out of her box and up to the last box, as she was making her way through the corridor, we would jump over the walls into her box. Bruja would then have to work out what to do; she couldn't turn around in the corridor so her only option was to go into the last box, turn and head back. Needless to say, as she was on the move we would climb back up the line of boxes to the last one and start all over again.

We of course thought this was hilarious, as to us Bruja looked stupid every time. The one thing Bruja wasn't was stupid. She fell for our trick several times and then worked out a way to catch us. One day as we called her she deliberately strolled out of her box, looking as nonchalant as possible whilst keeping one eye on us. Susan and I, howling with laughter at how we had tricked her again started to make our way down to the last box. We didn't notice Bruja slowing down and watching us. Her timing was perfect; just as we were passing her she did a quick about turn in the doorway and rushed back to her own box, firmly beating us to it. Susan and I were stunned by her ingenuity. It wasn't a fluke that she had waited till our backs were turned and we were too busy laughing before she doubled back. Needless to say we never caught her out again with that game.

"A horse should be obedient enough to stand in its box even if the door is open. It should not try to walk out," Carol would say to me. I thought quietly to myself about the games we had been playing with Bruja and didn't hold out much hope of success in teaching her this bit of obedience. I opened the door to her stable while she was eating her hay. I would leave the door open at all times when I was working with her, making sure I was between her and the open door. Once or twice she would make her way to the doorway just to look out. "Stand Bruja," would be the command. Surprisingly it didn't take her long to work out that she wasn't allowed to venture out of her box unless I said it was OK. This seemed to be going enormously well, too well in fact. One day, as I was making up feeds I realised that I had forgotten to close the latch on Bruja's door. "It's OK," I thought to myself, "she won't go anywhere." No sooner had the thought passed my mind than I heard the sedate clip clop of a horse walking down the corridor towards the open door. As Bruja was the only horse there it didn't take someone with the IQ of Einstein to work out who it was. Bruja came into the yard, looking for her feed. Before I could make it to the rescue she had taken herself for a canter through the yard owner's prize vegetable patch! I looked on in horror at the carnage she was inflicting among the cabbages and quickly shook her feed bucket, "Come on, come and get your dinner!" Whinnying with hunger she trotted happily out of the potatoes and across the yard. Again I had the unpleasant task of explaining myself to the owners, who surprisingly took it rather well. I learned my lesson that day of always bolting a stable door, no matter how well trained your horse may be

Within the first few months of Bruja being at her new home she managed to get into a fight with another horse and was rewarded with a nasty kick to her hock joint. Her whole hock swelled up and she was very lame. Once again I turned to Carol for advice. "OK let's do some hot and cold fomentation and serious cold hosing." She showed me how to soak stable bandages in hot water and apply them to the swollen leg. Bruja was too lame to object much to this treatment and when she started to lift her leg, Carol simply picked up her front foot to make her stand. Once the hot bandages had cooled we took them off and replaced them with bandages that had been soaked in cold water. This increase and decrease of temperature increased and decreased blood supply to the injured area. This allowed a fresh supply of nutrients to the tissues in order to repair the damage and a constant traffic of blood away from the tissues taking debris and damaged cells off for destruction. This was where I started to learn about first aid and minor ailments in horses. After a period of standing in for two days applying the bandages, Bruja had them taken off and her leg was looking a lot better. Because the fluid in the joint had gone down she could flex her leg and wasn't as lame.

"Now we need to hose her leg for twenty minutes

at a time," said Carol. Up until this point Bruja had never seen a hose or ever been washed. Fortunately the tap for the hose was in the corridor, which was too narrow for her to turn around in. She was still too sore to put up much of a resistance and after a few minutes she resigned herself to the fact that she was going to have to tolerate freezing water on her leg whether she liked it or not. All of the hours that I spent at the yard were dedicated towards curing Bruja's sore leg. I would patiently hose, bandage and massage her leg. Sitting on an upturned bucket by her side, I would talk to her, trying to cheer her up. After a week of treatment she was walking almost sound, although there was still some fluid in the joint. "OK we'll put her back out into the field. The best thing for her is to walk about and use her leg, which will clear the fluid better than anything." I hung on every word of Carol's sage-like advice

True enough after a further week of rest in the field Bruja's leg was back to normal and she could resume work. I had successfully learned how to treat a kick to the hock joint. Today your vet might use anti-inflammatory drugs to help reduce swelling, but in Bruja's day, the old-fashioned remedies were all that was available. They were just as effective, certainly cost less but required one important ingredient, something that Carol pointed out to me once Bruja was sound, "You did well there Morag, the best thing to cure an injury is a caring owner. Someone who is prepared to take their time to help their animal get better through the simplicity of the application of love and kindness. Patience and love is all you'll ever need."

Ride outs at the weekend were a highlight for us. If Susan were around we would ride to the main road, through the housing scheme where we would visit both our houses. It was a two-mile jaunt along main roads and a further mile or so through the schemes. When we were not on Bruja we would either cycle or walk. All my life I had imagined what it would be like to ride my own horse around the housing scheme, showing her off to all and sundry. Because I was so proud of Bruja it never occurred to me that she should be afraid of anything and I think this confidence on my part gave

Bruja an equal air of confidence and sense of adventure. She was a big hit with the neighbours and everyone around would come out of the houses to feed and pat the horse. She was coaxed up many a driveway with the promise of a carrot or a biscuit and even when she disgraced herself occasionally by eating the flowers it was all taken in good humour. It was quite probably the best education a young horse could get. Everyone welcomed Bruja and because nobody really knew anything about horses, they had no reason to be afraid of her. Children ran and shouted along the street cheering when she arrived on their patch. Mothers put babies onto her back for a photograph whilst toddlers ran about her feet. The air of trust and relaxation around her was all that Bruja needed for reassurance and of course the promise of something nice to eat!

One day I rode to my house for something to eat. I nonchalantly tied Bruja by her bridle no less, to the clothes pole in the back green, and left her munching whilst I went indoors for a ham sandwich. It never occurred to me or to Bruja, for that matter, that any harm could come of the situation - and thankfully nothing ever happened that we lived to regret.

Bruja experienced all manner of interesting things in her early years and it left her in good stead. There was virtually nothing that she hadn't seen or done.

One time Susan and I were outside her house when it suddenly started raining quite hard. "Quick, into the garage!" shouted my Uncle John. Bruja was unceremoniously ushered into a dark and cramped garage to wait till the rain went off. She never objected to this treatment; in fact she took it all in her stride.

Often Bruja would make the trip out to visit my Gran who stayed in a housing area called Sandyhills. To get there we travelled through Mount Vernon, along Sandyhills Road and into Gelston Street where my Gran stayed. All of the streets were main roads with cars, buses and lorries whizzing past. When we arrived Bruja would content herself with grazing the lawn, leaning over the rickety fence as I passed her carrots handed down to me by Gran. One day Susan and I tried to persuade Bruja to come up a set of steep stone steps and through the narrow gate leading into Gran's garden. She negotiated the steps no problem but when we got to the top we discovered she was too wide to go through the gate. Getting back down the steps was much harder than going up but Bruja gamely managed.

After visiting Gran we would often continue through Baillieston Main Street, passing through Barrachine traffic lights and trotting past Garrowhill on our journey back down Hangman's Brae to our stable yard near Calderpark Zoo. This would give Bruja an average round trip of about ten miles and she would travel this regularly throughout the summer months. What makes these ventures most extraordinary is the fact that Bruja was only around four years old and let's face it she had a mad woman on her back and occasionally another mad woman riding a bike along side.

Because she was kept in a built up area, Bruja and I soon realised the potential of any convenient grass verges. I would set off in canter along any bit of green I could find, no matter how narrow, and some were only as wide as the horse's two front feet. Bruja quickly learned that she could canter as long as she was on the soft green verge and would be pulled up sharply if she strayed onto the hard black road. In later years, as a result of our early desperate sprinting along roads, people would often remark at how good I was at keeping Bruja on the grass verges which were luxury to her as they were more than one foot wide. What they didn't know was that Bruja did all the work herself, being drawn to the green like a nail to a magnet and staying put just so she could move at speed. Anyone who keeps a horse under these circumstances will sympathise with the lengths Susan and I would go to just find a bit of land along which to run. Although her stable was in a green belt I'm afraid there was simply more belt than green and if any unsuspecting farmer forgot to put a gate on their hay field or barley field then they were fair game as far as we were concerned. We never ran across crops, we weren't that daft, but as soon as the harvest was in and before the field could be ploughed, you could guarantee the word would spread around the local horse riding kids and all and sundry would flock to the area just to have a gallop.

Playing fields, land being cleared for development, local parks and small pockets of woodland were obvious places to play. Actually the woodland was completely misnamed as it consisted of a few trees, some sandpits and a blade of grass. All have been sprinted across by Bruja and me at one time or another. We would even risk being caught by the curators of Bothwell Castle and try to find tracks through their woods that could be cantered along safely for more than a few strides.

As I look back I realise now that the element of fun and adventure instilled in Bruja in those early years is what gave her a zest for life and love of work. I was schooling her without even knowing it, in the best way possible, it was always a game. She learned how to run straight and true, stop quickly, turn on a sixpence, leap over small obstacles, stand quietly at traffic lights, ignore traffic and look innocent when faced by a Park Attendant, and all in the early years of her working life.

Dark Days

During the summer holidays just after my "O" grade exams I had my first real riding accident.

During the previous winter, when Bruja had just turned five, I decided that she should learn how to jump. In those days if you wanted to compete at all with horses then show jumping was really the only field to get into. Dressage was rare and very expensive. Eventing or Cross-Country were also well beyond the ways and means of our budget. Long Distance Riding was unheard off as was Western Riding.

The only things that we could afford to participate in were pony club games, a real handicap with a fifteen point two hands high horse or jumping. With Carol's help and guidance we nurtured within Bruja the love of jumping. She had a lot of natural talent, but was not keen on exerting the amount of energy needed to get over a fence.

We began by teaching her to trot over poles on the ground. Once she had grasped this concept and didn't try to leap over the whole lot or run around the edges we progressed to introducing her to a real fence. Two small road traffic cones were placed at the end of a line of trotting poles and the ends of two of the poles were balanced on their tops to make an X-shaped jump. The height of the "fence" in the middle was lucky to have been six inches, but this is more than enough for a young horse, which will learn all it needs to take it forward.

An odd thing, the peculiar relationship that horse-owning people have with traffic cones! In almost every yard you will see an interesting collection of these objects. They are extremely versatile for horse training purposes and I often wonder where they have all come from. Are there vast stretches of road around the country that have fewer cones on them than perhaps they started with?

After several initial setbacks with our jumping plans, Bruja eventually decided that she really quite liked this game and began to show a real talent.

During the summer after my "O" grades I was pottering about the field popping Bruja over some fences that had been left up by previous liveries. By this time Bruja and I were leaping over a staggering two feet height with confidence and thoroughly enjoying ourselves at the same time. On this particular afternoon I was just finishing off work and decided to pop over a small one-foot high fence. The pole was resting on the tops of two small barrels. Either my attention wasn't on the job, or Bruja was getting tired and just didn't jump high enough, we will never know. As we came up, Bruja's front legs hit the pole. Normally if the pole was fixed to proper jumping wings there wouldn't have been any problem, but as she hit the pole it rolled along with her across the top of the barrels, tangling up in her legs. She landed on her head with a thud, flipping over across her back and onto the ground. As Bruja's head hit the floor, I was propelled out of the saddle and thumped onto the grass. I was a little dazed but remember thinking, "I'm alright," and I was up until the point that Bruja flipped over and landed on me. I wriggled out from under her belly and lay for a moment trying to make sense of the spinning world around me.

Bruja lay still too, the wind knocked out of her. I felt her back legs across my thighs, in my mind, it was as if I was looking down at this scene and I could hear my own voice telling me "Move her legs out of the way in case she stands on you." With my left arm I grabbed her leg and started a push and shove argument with her. Bruja had decided that it was time to get up and didn't appreciate me hindering her attempts by shoving her hind legs away. I managed to slip my legs out from under her kicking hooves as she struggled to her feet. Sighing with relief I lay flat on the ground for a moment to get my breath back. Bruja was standing a few feet from me, still dazed and uncertain.

I sat up and immediately knew there was something seriously wrong. My whole left arm sloped downwards out of control, my shoulder sagging. I grabbed my left arm and lifted it up across my chest as I lay back down. Here was a real problem. As far as I knew I was the only one up at the yard at the time. I was in a field alone with no way to raise help. There was nothing for it, I would have to lie here and wait for someone to come along! Just as I was resigning myself to a long wait I saw three heads cautiously peer over the hedge. With relief I shouted out, "Excuse me! Help!" My rescuers came bounding to my aid.

I was taken to hospital and diagnosed with a broken collarbone and concussion. Bruja appeared to be fine, nothing more than a bloody nose and a headache, but as she recovered she began to show signs of a condition called "stringhalt". This is like a nervous twitch in the back legs as one or both of the legs are snatched up slightly higher than normal. It doesn't always appear in every stride, but can degenerate as the animal gets older. This condition is sometimes caused by injuries to the back and in Bruja's case it seems that this accident had damaged more than was first apparent. Although she never lost the twitch it was only ever apparent in walk, never trot and never canter As my abilities as a rider improved I was able to ask Bruja to lift her back and free her quarters in order to move better. When she did this she never once showed any signs of stringhalt. In retrospect I believe that she must have had some kind of trapped nerve in her back that might have been freed once her spine was arched and lifted.

Needless to say Bruja's confidence in jumping was greatly affected by this accident and as I was unable to ride it was up to Susan to re-train her. Full marks to Susan's diligence and perseverance. Bruja would refuse to jump even the tiniest of fences, sometimes even refusing to go over poles lying on the ground. Who could blame her really, she had received a bad fright, but it was important that we help her regain her self-confidence. Susan was put through the wringer. She was dumped unceremoniously over fences; she had her leg jammed between a horse and jump wing as Bruja ducked round the side. She had been thrown up the neck of the horse as Bruja hesitated only then to leap several feet higher than necessary over the fence. Over a period of time Bruja's confidence returned, largely due to the shouting, cursing and smacking she received if she didn't go over the fence. Once she had started to jump again she began to enjoy herself and overcame any fear of fences. The one good thing to come from the accident was that it taught Bruja to respect poles and she would always jump at least a foot higher than the actual fence and virtually never knocked a pole down in the whole of her jumping career. Quite an achievement in light of what she eventually attained.

After sitting my "O"grades and Higher exams I was offered a choice of careers. Go to University and study Genetics, go to Art School and study Graphic Design, go to Veterinary School and train to be a vet or work with horses. Much to the dismay of my Mother I chose the latter and embarked on a career with the animals I loved most. I was to begin my training as a British Horse Society Assistant Instructor or BHSAI at a school in Rue. During the summer after my exams and before I went to Rue I was plagued by ill health. My temper was so short I must have been appalling to be near. I was constantly exhausted and generally felt lousy. Bruja, I'm ashamed to say, bore the brunt of my frustration.

One day I brought Bruja in from the field. She was

walking sound but there were small bubble-like swellings at the base of each tendon, front and back. It was a very hot summer and I didn't know if the condition was caused by the heat. Carol examined the horse and assured me that it wasn't serious, just something called "Windgalls". She advised that I rest Bruja and if the swellings hadn't gone down in a few days to call the vet. In a moment of stupidity, furious at Bruja for deliberately making her legs swell, I threw her back into the field. Not surprisingly, after a few days she was no better and I called the vet. He examined her and announced that she had strained all her tendons and would need to be rested for a week with a new type of poultice applied to her legs twice a day. This was the first time that "Animalintex" had been brought onto the market and it was a godsend for those of us who had struggled with bran, bread and milk, kaolin and various other poultices. My frustration and anger boiled away inside of me. Bruja was a young, now seven year old, fit horse, which, not feeling sore in any way, objected to being kept cooped up in glorious weather and handled by a moody owner who punished her for the slightest misdemeanour.

On the last day of the application of the poultice I took her outside to change her bandages. I was on the last leg and had her tied to the five bar steel gate to the field. She fidgeted as I removed the last of the packing and I stood up quickly shouting, "Stand Up Straight!" slapping her hard on her neck. That was the last straw for Bruja. She threw her head up, pulling the rope tight and lifting the gate right off its hinges. I was smacked in the back by the gate and knocked flat as Bruja, terrified by this strange beast attached to her head, decided to leg it up the road. Fortunately the rope snapped as she spun round and I was left lying under the gate watching a trail of dust as Bruja disappeared through the yard. I couldn't run after her straight away, as I had to fix the gate before any of the horses escaped I prayed as I ran up the road that Bruja's good sense would prevail and she would stop when she reached level with the horses in the field. Fortunately that is just what she did. As I caught up with her it dawned on me that it was my bad temper that had caused this accident and that if Bruja had seriously hurt herself it was my fault. I would never have forgiven myself. Much to my relief Bruja was perfectly OK and when I related the story to Carol that night she commented, "Can't be much wrong with her legs if she can run about with a gate swinging from her head." So, despite the fact that the small round swellings were still there, I started working Bruja again and letting her back out into the field. Over the years the swellings did finally disappear and only in really hot weather did her legs become slightly puffy around the ankles.

As the time drew closer for me to leave to train for my BHSAI it was becoming more and more apparent to all that I was not my usual self. I found my temper becoming even shorter and I seemed to be permanently exhausted. After the incident with the gate if I found myself losing the rag with Bruja I would walk away and literally count to twenty before I came back. For some reason it seemed that Bruja became quite disobedient at this time. She seemed to be constantly misbehaving.

Whether she sensed my own emotional and physical weakness and deliberately tested my authority or whether she was behaving normally and I was making a mountain out of a molehill I'll never know, but I can honestly say it was a dark time in our friendship and tested all of our bonds to their very limit.

We left the yard in September and arrived in Rue to begin our training. It was a standard course for a working pupil. Each morning there were forty horses to be mucked out, fed, hayed, watered and groomed. Two other working pupils plus the head girl of the yard and myself did all the chores.

In return for teaching lessons and working on the yard we were trained for our exams. It is a standard arrangement that is still in place today. I learned a lot from my time in Rue and gained valuable riding experience. However, I would be a liar to say that I enjoyed myself. I was very depressed and unhappy. The work was gruelling and typically with three teenage girls living together there was a fair amount of ganging up. I found myself on the outside of the threesome and instead of taking advantage of the learning opportunities for myself and Bruja I simply took out my frustrations on the animal that loved me.

I didn't know what was wrong with me until my Mum decided to make an appointment for me to visit the Doctor on my day off. We worked six days a week with a Monday off and every third Sunday we had a half-day. On the Monday I went to see the Doctor and the following Monday it was diagnosed that I had been suffering from Glandular Fever but that the worst was past and I should now be on the mend. Unfortunately by this time my relationship with the yard owners and other girls had been strained beyond repair and I was looking for an alternative yard closer to home.

My next-door neighbour had asked me to come and look at a horse she was thinking of buying. It was kept in a yard outside Strathaven. This yard was a livery and riding school and had a large and prestigious clientele. It was at that time the largest equestrian centre in Scotland. Gleneagles had not yet been built, and as soon as I walked onto the yard I knew I wanted to work there. The horse my neighbour was looking at was young and inexperienced but had the potential to be a super little jumping mare. I advised her to buy it for the princely sum of £800 plus tack and rugs. As it turned out it was the best investment she ever made.

I started to make enquiries as to whether or not the yard would take on working pupils. The yard owner kindly agreed to meet with my Mum and me on one of my Mondays off. I was disappointed to learn that the yard had never taken on any working pupils and the owner didn't feel that they had the teaching experience necessary to complete my training. My Mum surprisingly leapt to my rescue. She suggested that I work at the yard five and half days a week for nothing and if she paid for my horse to be kept on Livery there, at that time an extremely expensive £30 per week, then that would cover any teaching fees. I was to have a lesson at least once a day from the Head Girl who when approached with the idea was delighted to be able to train someone for their exams. If at the end of the four-month period I passed my AI then I would commence employment at the yard for the going rate of £30 per week. It was the opportunity of a lifetime! The yard owner was happy, my Mum was happy and I, for the first time in a long while, was happy too. The only drawback was that I had to leave Bruja in Rue for a week whilst a box became free for her on the yard. I was anxious about what might happen to her when I told the yard owners in Rue that I was leaving. I asked one of the livery clients on the yard to keep an eye on her for the week, for despite my bad temper and unforgivable behaviour towards Bruja, she was the most important thing in the world to me and I would have gladly died for her. Bruja in return, despite the numerous hard times she had received was still kind and gentle and relied on me heavily for support, for she too was desperately unhappy in the yard. I was glad that the livery watched her for me. Although she wasn't ill-treated in any way, her box wasn't mucked out as well as it ought to have been and she hadn't been groomed or had her feet picked out for a full week.

The livery client volunteered to bring Bruja down

to Strathaven for me, an act of kindness for which I will eternally be grateful.

A Team Is Made

The years spent at Lethame House Equestrian Centre were a great education and great fun for me. I was finally able to do the one thing I always wanted. I passed my exams with no problems and went on to work as an instructor at the centre. I gained invaluable experience in schooling many types of different animals and dealing with their individual characters. It never seemed as though I was working because I enjoyed everything I did. It was like being allowed to do your favourite thing every day of the week. It would be wrong to say that it was easy; in fact it was very hard work with up to ten livery and school horses to be looked after by each member of staff. The standards laid down by the yard for care of the horse was very high and the policy of selling the school horse on after two years of work in the lessons meant that there were always new animals to train and school.

I met many different horse characters in those years that all have stories surrounding them, but this is Bruja's story and I shall concentrate on her.

The day Bruja moved onto the yard she immediately began to cheer up. I was much happier and settled and she began to regain her old confidence in me. Together we were trained by various head girls and external instructors and Bruja began to show a serious ability and interest in show jumping. There was always an opportunity to compete at the yard and shows were in abundance. We initially started to compete in unaffiliated jumping. The fences were no larger than three feet six inches and it gave ample experience to both me and Bruja in a competition that had less pressure. Because of her early schooling Bruja had learned to judge her own stride into a fence. That meant she could judge for herself where the best place would be to take off. I would always try to place her in just the right position, but if I ever got it wrong Bruja would correct me and take off where she knew best.

It never ceased to amaze people who saw her jump. "That horse jumps like a pony," was the most common expression I heard. What they meant was that most horses rely on their riders to place them at the fence and get it right. Very few have the ability to correct a rider's mistake. Ponies, on the other hand, have a very strong sense of self-preservation and rely mainly on their own judgement on where to take off. With Bruja it was very much a team effort, which was born out of mutual respect and understanding. My job was to get her to the fence; her job was to get over it. However, if I got it wrong Bruja would correct as much as she could. Sometimes though it was not possible for her to correct my mistake and she knew that it would be safer and better for her to refuse to jump. My horse and friend was brave and courageous only because she knew that if all else failed she could stop. Bruja was never afraid to jump and never afraid to stop. Very few show jumpers today are not afraid to stop because of what would happen to them if they did. Most would rather risk life and limb by jumping a fence when wrong rather than face the wrath of their riders if they dared stop. This makes for a dangerous animal to ride, one, which has become a machine that jumps out of fear and not joy - an animal that can no longer think for itself or for its rider. I would never punish Bruja for refusing a fence. I always gave her the benefit of the doubt. I trusted her judgement and her love of jumping. I knew she would never miss out on a chance to jump a fence if she could.

After her first year of unaffiliated jumping at Lethame House she walked away with all the trophies in her class, winning the championship and bringing honour to the yard. It was suggested to me that I register Bruja and compete in the affiliated season the following year. This I did and Bruja exceeded all of my expectations.

This was the beginning of an understanding and deep respect that Bruja and I had for each other. She was a mature horse of ten years of age and a character in her own right. We were very close friends. I loved Bruja more than words could say. I trusted her with my life and she trusted me with hers. When we were schooling in the arena we became so close that I only had to think the command and she would carry out my instructions. I am a great believer in this. I tried to ride

Bruja out every other day and we spent our time galloping around having fun. I always tried to instil the same element of excitement in her life, never boring her with constant work and only jumping her once a week, even if there was a competition on at the weekend. I was not afraid to admit that this form of communication went two ways. It wasn't the first time that when out on what was supposed to be a quiet hack that the sudden urge to gallop came across me. I would follow Bruja's eye line and we would discover an open gate to a secluded field with no "witnesses" to our crime of running. If I glanced at something then Bruja's head would also turn in that direction. We worked together as one. We were a team.

It would be misleading to say that we didn't have any arguments. We were both strong willed females with minds of our own. Quite often we didn't see eye to eye and Bruja would make me work to get the results I wanted. If I said chalk she quite often would say cheese. But as soon as we entered the arena to compete, all arguments were forgotten, the team fused together and performed at their best.

Some people work all of their lives to achieve the oneness that Bruja and I had. I respected Bruja for what she was. She wasn't a human being; she didn't think like a human, she didn't have the same values and beliefs that humans have. Bruja was a horse. She thought like a horse, she acted like a horse; she was wise and gentle as only a horse can be. She was special and it took a long time for me to realise that it was simply because I understood her mind, her ideals and values and accepted them, that we were so close. She was intelligent and intuitive in the way that horses are. She understood that I was not like her and that I didn't think like her and she was patient with me when I misunderstood what she meant. I did not impose human characteristics on her nor expect her to behave like a human. Likewise she did not impose equine characteristics on me and didn't expect me to behave like a horse.

Best in Scotland

Although our work at Lethame House was hard and continuous, I still had time to spend with Bruja. We had grown as close as was physically possible for two such different creatures. Although not a demonstrative horse, Bruja would spend time just to be by my side and rest her head on my back or shoulder in friendly contemplation. In return many private moments were shared with Bruja as I would stroke and caress her, talking to her quietly about this and that. I remember the surprise of one of our livery clients as she leaned over the door chatting to me as I plaited Bruja's mane for a competition the next day. So close was the mutual understanding between Bruja and me that I sensed her agitation as she stood patiently to be plaited. "What is it hen?" I asked. Bruja rolled her eye back towards me flicking an ear to the water bucket and blowing softly through her nose. "Do you want a drink?" An almost imperceptible nod of her head gave me all the answer I needed. "OK, but move slowly. I don't want to waste any of the plaits and make sure you come back to be finished." I unclipped the rope from her head collar and she very carefully moved around me (I was standing on an upturned bucket), took a long drink from her bucket and returned to her original position for me to finish the job. The livery client looked on, utterly astounded. "If I hadn't seen that with my own eyes I wouldn't have believed it!" "Oh," I replied calmly, "Bruja understands most of what is said to her so you should be careful what you say."

I remember a funny incident that happened at Lethame not long after I had started there. Bruja had always lain down in front of me. She had no fear of humans and trusted me completely. Quite often when she was younger she would lie in her box and I would come in and sit with her. When she lay flat out and fell fast asleep she would begin to snore in a rather odd manner. Bruja had a habit of holding her breath! She would inhale with a snort then begin to exhale with a groan. Halfway through exhaling she would hold her breath suddenly and you would be on tender hooks till she suddenly gasped the last lungful of air out before starting again. If you didn't know her you would have thought she was in agony. Anyway, I had just got home from the yard one day when I received an alarming phone call. "Come back to the yard quick, Bruja's very ill, we've called the vet," were the words I heard. I jumped back into my car and rushed to the yard. It was usually a thirty minutes' drive and I did it in twenty minutes. When I got to the yard there was a group of rather shamefaced people, an irritated vet and Bruja looking innocently over her door. "What's wrong?" I asked. "Just after you left tonight Bruja went down in her box and started groaning in agony," was the immediate response. "Did she inhale, groan, hold her breath then snort?" I asked. "Yes," was the amazed reply. "Oh that's alright, that was her just snoring." "But she wouldn't get up, even when we went in and tried to lift her!" was the even more amazed response "I know, once Bruja has decided to go for a sleep you can't persuade her otherwise and she won't budge for anyone." The vet laughed and explained that it was unusual for a horse to lie down in front of anyone for any length of time and even more unusual for them to be trusting enough not to be afraid, even when people enter their box. I was surprised myself. I didn't know that horses didn't usually lie down in front of people. I was so used to it with Bruja that I assumed it was normal. In fact one day she lay down in the field and wouldn't get up for me to catch her. I had to walk away and come back after an hour once she had woken up!

I remember coming into the yard one morning and noticing with surprise that Bruja's head wasn't poking over her door watching for me. "Morag, can I see you for a minute?" the yard owner shouted me into the house. "Bruja has escaped during the night. The stable door that opens onto the back passage was ajar and the door at the end of the passage was left open. You can go out in your car and look for her." I listened in stunned silence, fear welling up inside me. There were a lot of farm roads around the yard, but they all eventually led to very busy main roads. I had visions of Bruja lying dead at the side of the road and that was the first time the realisation that I just might lose her hit me.

I jumped in my car and drove frantically from farm to farm, asking if anyone had seen a black horse. As my questions were met with polite nos and concerned looks, I was almost beside myself with fear. I truly thought I had lost her, my friend and companion, my partner. I returned to the yard after almost two hours of fruitless searching. The only consolation I had was that no one had heard of any road accidents concerning a horse. My boss met me at the gate. "We've found her," she said smiling, " A lady who owns a stud farm three miles away found her in her yard last night chatting up her stallion. She caught her and put her in a box for the night till she found the owners. Get your saddle and bridle, I'll drive you over and you can ride her back." I broke into tears of relief and I realised my beautiful Bruja was safe. The kind woman who owned the stud farm thought it was very funny. "Your horse is nothing but a tart!" she said laughing as she led me to Bruja's temporary home, "Just as well the stallion was locked in his box otherwise you might have got a wee surprise in eleven months' time!" It was blatantly obvious that Bruja had planned the whole affair perfectly. I had ridden past this very farm on several occasions, but it wasn't part of my regular route. Bruja had known exactly where she was heading that night she escaped. I reckon she'd fancied that stallion for quite some time.

Bruja was the master of practical jokes, she could innocently set up a situation to make you look stupid or to infuriate you but always managed to look as though it had simply happened! One such classic "accidental incident" was played out on my friend Sharon. On a fine mid-summers day Bruja and I had been competing in a yard in Carluke and while enjoying the warmth of the afternoon sun we were watching the last of the jump offs. Sharon had been grooming for me that day and had just sat down with a much wanted and much deserved cup of tea which was paid for with the last of our money. She was just about to take a sip from the steaming mug as she watched the last horse jump round when Bruja slowly and calmly leaned over her shoulder and snorted the biggest, greenest bogey you could imagine right into her cup! Sharon stared in utter disbelief as the rest of us fell about laughing with Bruja gazing off into the distance trying very hard to look as though she hadn't meant it at all! Poor Sharon, she was I'm afraid the butt of Bruja's jokes on more than one occasion.

I registered Bruja with the British Show jumping Association under the really imaginative name of Bruja! Our professional career was starting. We were in with the big boys now.

In those days if you won a class you received a whole £10s (entry fees were usually £2). The first class you started in was Newcomers. Once your horse had won £50 you couldn't compete in Newcomers and had to progress to Foxhunter. With £200 on your card you were out of Foxhunter and competed in Grade C's. After Grade C was Grade B then Grade A. Grade A was the really big money and the fences were enormous.

Bruja jumped at least once a week in competition and we won the first five Newcomer classes from the day she was eligible. This meant that after only five classes in BSJA competition Bruja had already won too much money and was forced to compete in the Foxhunter classes. As the classes progressed the fences got bigger. Foxhunter maximum height was four feet two inches and width I think was about four feet six inches. To jump Bruja was to fly. She was wonderful. As you approached the fence she would accelerate. I knew and she knew that to cover the bigger fences she needed a little more miles per hour. She did not have the scope of a German bred horse nor was she a rangy thoroughbred. Her skill was in turning and springing. She was smart too. My job was to get her to the fence. I always tried my best to place her in just the right spot, but sometimes I got it wrong. This was when our mutual understanding and deep friendship came into play. Bruja would sense instantly that I was unsure and she would take over and adjust her stride accordingly. She liked to be in deep at her fences. Technically (according to the textbooks!) she was too close to her fences on take off. But I knew that Bruja could jump six feet straight up if she wanted to, but she struggled to jump a four foot by four foot parallel because she was short in the back and couldn't stretch out over the fence.

My soul mate and I jumped at least once a week BSJA for over two years and in all that time it is a credit to her that I can say I can count on one hand the number of poles down or stops she gave me in all that time. I think there was only one instance when she didn't get placed or win her class. That is a very hard record to match.

I remember once when her skill at turning was so dramatically demonstrated. We were in the jump-off of a big class. It was a Grade C, a small Open. The course builder had designed an excellent course, which tested the skill of the rider and horse combination and not the jumping ability of the horse. In other words, those riders who worked and placed their horses correctly and whose horses responded willingly would succeed. Often you see a superb horse with an inexperienced rider on its back. A lazy or unskilled rider would not be able to make the turn or count the strides and they would fail. The one point where time was saved required a left-hand turn after a large upright and onto a nice ascending spread. Most people were opting to go round a fence that happened to be in the way of the turn, but I knew that if Bruja started to turn in the air then she could get to the inside of the other fence and still have plenty of time for the spread. As I approached the fence and gave Bruja the signal that we would be turning left quickly. She took off, arching her back up to meet me. I dropped my weight onto my left leg and leaned into her left shoulder, bringing my left leg onto her side to support the bend and brushing my right leg behind the girth, asking her to move away. She wrapped herself round my leg and swung to the left. We landed turning and easily slipped between the two fences. Unfortunately Bruja turned so well and quickly that my foot caught the wing of the jump and knocked it down! I may have got four faults, but I also received a big cheer from the crowd.

I remember vividly the people who became involved in Bruja's life and who knew her. My main claim to fame was when Stephen Hadley gave a course at Lethame House. At the end of the week he walked up to me and said, "What a super little horse. Will you sell her?" I was flattered and proud as punch but needless to say the answer was no. Everyone who saw Bruja was amazed at her ability and the apparent ease with which she jumped. One man in particular constantly upped his offer price for her after each class she won. He confronted me one day and offered a ridiculous sum of money for her. I laughed and said, "Look Davie, she isn't worth that kind of money and besides she's my friend and you don't sell your friends." He laughed good-naturedly and accepted defeat. One of my biggest compliment givers was none other than Mr Billy Stewart himself. "By God lassie," he would say as I beat yet another of his 'Big show jumpers' into second place, "I must have been sleeping the day I sold you that hoss!"

While she was at Lethame House I had the opportunity to take her to the beach for the first time. Bruja was bundled into the horsebox along with most of the livery clients and school horses that had been hired for the event, and we set off. When we got to the beach Bruja stood in wonder, gazing at the sea. Whether she had ever seen such an expanse of water before, I didn't know (she was supposed to have originally come from Ireland and was shipped across in a job lot. Perhaps she was looking for boats!). Anyway she was so engrossed that she stood like an angel waiting to be tacked up. The sound of gulls carried on the breeze as we set off in a nice easy jog along the beach to warm her up. She spooked at the seaweed and snorted at the waves as the foam broke upon the shore, but she kept her line as straight as possible. When we turned round after the one-mile trot, she suddenly realised that this entire expanse of sand was for her personal use and without any prompting on my part we lunged forward into a full gallop leaving the others standing in our wake as sand kicked up from Bruja's hooves as they sped across the damp surface. It was the first time that I had ever really let Bruja fly as fast as she wanted for as long as she wanted. She was very fast for a non-thoroughbred. No other horse in the yard could catch her. She could stay as well, running the mile, flat out almost all the way. It was the most exhilarating experience of my life. Nothing can beat it; nothing can touch it. After running once, it was all that I could do to keep Bruja in a sensible trot. Despite her hard breathing she insisted on trying to leap away every second stride, or spin in circles, bunny hopping into a canter. She loved to run. Finally, as a result of frustration more than anything else, I headed her into the sea. I thought that she would probably refuse to go in and that this would keep her occupied long enough for her to catch her breath. How wrong I was. Without a moments hesitation she trotted into the waves, snorting at the strange feeling of the water dragging her legs as the beach gave way to the ocean. She fell into a bouncy slow motion trot and carried on regardless, delighting in the experience. I headed straight out, wanting to see just how far she would go. Finally, she was too deep to trot and started to swim! The feeling of this wonderful animal swimming beneath me was the weirdest sensation. Her breathing came in strange moaning snorts as she blew excess water away from her nostrils. I floated behind, clinging onto the saddle as she glided effortlessly along while the waves broke around us and foam rushed toward the land. She swam in a large arc, sensibly heading toward the beach. As soon as her legs got a hint of the solid ground beneath, she set off, galloping as soon as she was free of the water sending a spray of sand and sea flying up behind her. The only way I could get her to stand still was to dismount and even then she paced excitedly around me. It is safe to say that Bruja loved to go to the beach. I was soaked through and getting colder by the minute but the excitement the ride and to see Bruja enjoying the moment was all the warmth I needed.

That evening we cleaned the tack with fresh water to remove the salt from the sea and Bruja and all those who had been on the ride slept soundly, the effects of an exhilarating day in the fresh sea air.

Bruja qualified for the Regional Finals two years in a row for Foxhunter and Newcomers. We competed amongst the best horses in Scotland and she won her chance to go to Wembley and compete at the prestigious Horse of the Year Show. The money required for such a competition was high. I knew I couldn't afford the transport, accommodation and entry fees. I was offered countless lifts by some of the top names in Scottish Show jumping and a place in their boxes, but I turned them down. My parents were struggling to keep Bruja and me. I was the highest paid groom in Scotland at the time and I earned £75 a week. My horse was kept for free, but all vet bills, vehicle expenses, digs money and blacksmith bills were carefully scraped from my earnings. I couldn't and wouldn't ask my parents for any more handouts. I knew they would have tried to raise the money, proud of my chance, but maybe I was a little scared about the whole thing. Maybe I felt it would just be too much for Bruja and me. I didn't go.

Bruja finally won too much money and was about to be upgraded to a Grade B. By this time she was getting older, she would have been twelve years old. Not a great age, but old enough to feel the height and width of the fences we were now required to jump. I am not a brave rider when it comes to jumping. All of my courage came from Bruja's love of the game, her joy of sailing easily over a fence. I would walk courses of fences that were higher than me and feel sick to my stomach. I knew that these fences were the limit of Bruja's ability. I knew that if I made any kind of mistake she wouldn't have enough spare to get out of trouble. I remember the words Carol first said to me when we were teaching Bruja to jump, "Promise me Morag that the day Bruja says no is the day you quit." I came into a fence in the jump off. The turn was sharp but not overly so, the fence not too big and the stride good. Bruja stopped. A thing she rarely did unless terribly wrong. I turned her away and took her in again. She stopped. I struck her once with the jumping stick and brought her round again. She jumped the fence and completed the course but she had said no. Enough was enough. That was my last class. I never competed BSJA again.

This was the time that changed my life. I contracted a rare lung condition called "Farm's Lung".

It meant I was severely allergic to moulds that live in hay or straw. My career with horses was over. I had to look for another job. While I searched Bruja was given a holiday along with a friend of ours and her horse called Lacy. Bruja and Lacy had the run of a 90-acre field in Quarter and they loved it. After four years of being stabled with no access to grazing and competing every weekend it must have seemed like heaven to her. I too enjoyed every moment. It seemed that in working so intensely with horses I had become jaded. Now though, I recaptured the intimate side of our relationship, the kind of understanding that we had with each other when we were both younger. Often I would simply jump on Bruja bareback and she would take me wandering around the hill, following the narrow cattle and sheep tracks, jumping over the small burns and gullies. I should mention that Bruja had no bridle or head collar. She was free to wander where she pleased and I was simply along for the ride. These moments were ours. This was where our mutual understanding and deep love for each other was fused.

I was her and she was me. We were the same. She would graze contentedly while I quietly stroked her soft hide or untangled her unruly tail. She never ran away, she never left me alone. When it was time for me to go she would walk with me to the gate to say goodnight and watch till I had got in my car before returning back up the slopes to join her friend Lacy.

The Dynamic Duo

I got a job working in a camera shop as a Sales Assistant and was earning enough money to keep Bruja without handouts from others. This was the start of the fun times again. I stabled Bruja in Dalziel estate in Motherwell. She was there for eight months during the winter, but once again there was no grazing available and so I began looking for somewhere else. During my stay there I would hack Bruja down to Strathclyde Park and ride at breakneck speed along all of the horse tracks. These hacks revitalised Bruja. It was a journey back to her youth when she and I would gallop at every excuse.

During the winter months when I had just clipped her, I rather stupidly took her for a fast hack around Strathclyde Park. She was perfectly well behaved right up to the point where I started galloping. As we approached a slight downhill stretch Bruja's head disappeared between her legs. I remember thinking, "Oh, no!" as I registered the dangerous position I was in. Before I could think, up came the back end of a spectacular buck. I didn't stand a chance. As I sailed past her head I shouted, "Stand still!" in the faint hope she would obey and wouldn't run away. Much to my surprise not only did it not hurt too much as I slammed into the ground but Bruja actually listened to me. She managed to stop in only a few strides and stood looking rather shamefaced (and not without a slight hint of amusement in her eyes) as I picked myself off the ground. Grumbling I caught her and jumped aboard setting her off in her gallop again (this time keeping my hands up and body a good bit straighter). It was the only time in her life that Bruja bucked me off and it was of course completely accidental, at least that's what I like to imagine!

I found a farm in Hamilton and moved her at the beginning of the year. To our surprise we met up with an old horse friend. She was one of the riding school horses from Lethame that had been sold on. Her name was Kerry and she and Bruja were old friends.

We spent two happy years at that farm. Bruja had as much grazing as she could wish for. The big disadvantage was that there was nowhere to ride in the winter. Knowing that Bruja was getting older and that she should be kept as fit as possible I would get up at 4.30am and drive thirty minutes to the farm. I then mucked out the stable, groomed Bruja, made up night feeds and hay nets and rode. I tried to time my riding to just about 6.30am when the roads were quiet. I wore fluorescent gear and hacked out on the dark country roads. We would trot for a couple of miles then make our way to a piece of wasteland and tracks where we would canter. Bruja was very sensible. She never galloped along the tracks in the dark; she knew better and kept a nice steady pace. We were back in the yard for 7.30am when I would feed her and put her out in the field for the day. I then got changed and went to work.

Once my days work had finished I would go back to the yard to bring her in. What a pleasure it was to bring her straight in to a nice clean stable and be able to give her a feed straight away. I looked on at the other D.I.Y. livery clients who rushed about at night mucking out and trying to get everything done. I used my time to clean and groom my horse.

I hadn't jumped Bruja over a single fence for almost two years when someone suggested that I try and see if she would like cross-country. I took her out into the big field and put up a small two foot show jump. I wondered if she would still want to jump at all let alone try something new. I hadn't taken her over any fences since that fateful class B.S.J.A. My fears were unjustified. Bruja wasn't afraid or resentful of jumping, she had merely needed a rest. She flew over the fence with all of her old gusto and my heart leaped in joy with hers. I began to jump her again once a fortnight just for fun. She never jumped anything over four foot in height and she did this with such ease that her confidence in her own abilities returned tenfold. For Bruja jumping was once again the highlight of her life, her reward, her special treat.

It was at this yard that I did one of the most stupid things I have ever done with any horse. The worst thing is I should have known better with my years of experience, but I was blind because it was

Bruja. I took her out one day to school her in the barley field. The soil was heavy clay and deep going. I thought it would be good to strengthen Bruja's legs. I schooled her for forty minutes. Bruja was brave and willing and although it must have been hell for her, she kept going. The next day I came up to the yard in the morning to put her out and of course she was crippled with strained tendons.

I called the vet straight away. He came out and examined her then said the worst thing I had ever heard. "Is she insured?" he asked. I gulped nervously and said, "Yes she is." "Well you better inform your insurance company because I don't know if she will come right." I was devastated, more so because it was my own stupidity that had caused this suffering and pain in my good friend. I swore that come what might, Bruja would be all right. I treated her the traditional way. Complete box rest for seven days with hot poulticing changed every twelve hours. She was put on painkillers and anti-inflammatory, but the rest was up to me. I had to do this right. I remembered the benefits of cold hosing, something that by now had gone out of fashion, so in between bandage changing I would sit with a bucket of ice cold water and sponge down her legs (she wasn't even allowed to move the short distance to the hose). It broke my heart to see her in so much pain. At one point her legs were so sore that if she moved the wrong way she would rear with the pain. After the week of poulticing came another week of support bandaging and the beginning of her short walks. At first I could only lead her out of her box to muck out and that was enough but by the end of the week we had progressed to walking for five minutes around the yard. She was still on painkillers so it was difficult to judge if she was really sound or not. By the end of the second week the course of painkillers had stopped. The vet came back out and examined her. This was the moment of truth. She had another week of walking to gradually build up her muscles, but this time the support bandages had to come off and she would only wear stable bandages when she was standing in. This was the time where her tendons could relapse and collapse again. If they did there would be no option but to put her down. If I cried once, I cried a thousand times and cursed myself for my own lack of common sense. Bruja, however, had no intentions about being put down. All those years of roadwork had hardened her tendons and they recovered completely. When the vet examined her for the final time I asked if I should always wear support bandages when she was being exercised. "Certainly not," said the vet, "Get her out on the roads and get those legs toughened up!" I had learned my lesson the hard way and would not put Bruja through that kind of pain again.

Once Bruja was fit I was given the chance to borrow a box and car and take her to the beach. One of my friends who helped me at the time came along too as she had never galloped Bruja. As usual, as soon as Bruja was out of the box she started pacing excitedly, unable to wait for her run. I had made the fatal mistake of wearing plain leather reins on her bridle. I rode her first, trying to keep to a steady trot/canter to warm her up. I noticed that the reins kept slipping as they became increasingly wet. Almost at the end of our warm up there was a small lagoon left by the tide. I pulled Bruja up and we slowly waded through it. It was shallow at first but quite suddenly got to a depth of about three foot. I made a mental note to pull her up on the way back. We got to the end of the stretch and turned to run back. Here is where I suddenly realised that leather reins were not a good idea. Bruja leapt away at top speed. I sat comfortably until we were approaching the lagoon. I pulled the reins and they simply slipped through my fingers, making not the slightest bit of difference to Bruja's speed. I started to frantically pull on the reins but they continually slipped away, seeming like slime in my fingers. I looked up and it was too late. Bruja hit the lagoon doing almost thirty miles an hour! We survived the first few feet of shallows, but as soon as she hit the deep water, down she went and I sailed over her head. If you have never fallen into water at speed you will not know how disorienting it is. I had managed to gulp a lung full of air before I was submerged, but I was terrified of Bruja suddenly landing on top of me and drowning me. I swam frantically in what I hoped was the opposite direction of Bruja and finally came up to the surface. I looked up the beach wondering where Bruja had got to when a puzzled snort from behind caused me to turn round. There she stood, totally bedraggled and bemused, water running out of her nose and ears, wondering who had snatched the ground away. I waded over to her and clambered aboard. We walked out of the lagoon. Had Bruja learned her lesson from this experience, not a bit of it. As soon as her feet struck sand she was off again, mad as ever. When it came to Sharon's turn to ride she thought she would play safe and take Bruja into the sea for a swim. She swam her out to a sand bank and walked the length of the (what was now two feet deep) water. Unfortunately, as soon as Bruja turned round she was off again and once more the slippery reins prevented Sharon from holding her back. Bruja was doing OK till she ran off the sand bank. Both she and Sharon disappeared completely under the sea. I stood on the shore thinking, "Oh my God, she's drowned my horse and herself!" There was absolutely nothing I could do. Just as I was really beginning to panic I saw Bruja emerge from the waves and a few moments later Sharon appeared, looking like the creature from the black lagoon with her jumper down to her ankles. She must have swum about twenty yards under water. Bruja made her way over to Sharon as she stood in the shallows. Sharon jumped back on board and surprise, surprise, as soon as she was on off went Bruja again. She just never learned!

Bruja recovered so well that one of the girls on the yard talked me into doing a novice Cross Country event and, on the assurances that the fences were all very low and quite easy, I decided to go. When I arrived I discovered that they were indeed very inviting fences. It was a one and a half mile course with thirty two fences to jump. I set off not quite knowing what Bruja would make of these types of fences. I needn't have worried. As soon as she realised that she was allowed to gallop AND jump she was off with the bit quite literally between her teeth. The only slight hesitation she gave was at the steps. A series of plateaus down a hill where the horse must drop onto one platform, take a step, then drop down to the next. She only stopped long enough to check the drop, hardly pausing in her stride. All of her experience as an early explorer and adventurer had stood her in good stead and she tackled the fences like a real pro. We finished the course in quite a spectacular time of one minute fifty four seconds!

The second time we did a Cross Country course was very nearly the last. I don't remember where it was exactly, but it was in the grounds of some Castle or other (that narrows it down!). There was no novice or intermediate classes that day for horses, only the open competition. I had walked the course earlier and there were no fences over four foot. Knowing that Bruja was still capable of jumping six foot I felt that it shouldn't be too hard.

We set off at a good pace. As we approached the fences I suddenly realised that a four foot show jump is very different from a four foot Cross Country fence.

These fences would not fall in if the horse hit them; the horse would fall instead. After the first couple of fences Bruja's blood was up and she was completely at ease with herself. I on the other hand was terrified. Once more I was in the situation where I couldn't make a mistake. I had to be right or I risked breaking not only my but Bruja's neck. We completed the course at a terrific rate. Bruja by this time had lost her enthusiasm for the Cross Country and was beginning to feel a little nervous herself. The last fence was what was called a bullfinch, four foot of solid fence with two foot of loose brush and branches. The horse was supposed to jump through the loose twigs, but Bruja of course was a show jumper; no one had explained to her the concept of brush fences. As we approached the fence, almost flat out, I felt her suddenly prop back and sit down on her hocks. I thought for a moment she was going to stop. The crowd gave a gasp and cheer and I let out a yell of surprise and panic as Bruja bunched her muscles and jumped clear over the fence. She leapt six foot straight up as usual! We carried on through the finish line and I remember someone shouted, "It's OK you're finished, you can stop kicking now!"

That event put me off Cross Country for good. For Bruja's sake we went back the following year to the small novice Cross Country that we had jumped first. She bounded round with all her old confidence restored. I don't know how she would have felt if she had been faced with the open course again though!

I remember two incidents at Dickson's Farm that are worth the telling. Bruja loved children. If there was a baby in a pram she would stop and let the clumsy little fingers prod about her face with all the patience in the world. One of the livery clients at the yard had a three-year old daughter. This child was not afraid of horses and knew what and what not to do around them. Bruja's stable door was open to allow fresh air to circulate and she had a chain across the doorway to prevent any escaping. I heard the little girl talking to Bruja as she patted her and I stuck my head round the corner to watch. As I stood at the end of the corridor my jaw dropped as I watched the scene unfold. Neither

Bruja nor the child was aware that I was there. Bruja had stuck her head under the chain so the little girl could pat her and this she did with great gusto. Bruja would then gently nudge her and look pointedly in her eyes, then look at the bales of hay across the corridor. After a few moments the little girl grasped what Bruja was saying. She ran over to the hay and grabbed as much as her small hands could carry and presented them to Bruja who then very carefully took the strands from her fingers. Once the hay was being munched the little girl would laugh at how clever she was to feed a horse. Bruja would then repeat the exercise. Look at the girl, look at the hay, look at the girl, and look at the hay. Each time the little girl waited till Bruja asked her for hay before she moved. It was the first time that I have ever seen a horse train a human!

Another incident which highlights the generous heart that Bruja had was when my next door neighbour's little girl asked if she could come and see the horse. Jade was only three at the time and so I asked her mum if this would be OK. So with mum's permission and a full warning to do exactly what Morag said, Jade came to the yard. She had never been near animals before, having no pets of her own, so was a bit overwhelmed with all of the horses and their great size. With Bruja however, she seemed more confident and Bruja, sensitive as always, was very gentle in her movements and very placid in her behaviour. Jade even sat on her back for a short walk (fifteen point two hands high is a long way up when you are only three years of age!!). Once Bruja had "worked" we took her back to her stable. I put her in her box with the chain across and told my tiny companion, "Now Jade, you stand there and watch Bruja for me while I make up her feeds. You mustn't go anywhere else, just stand there." Jade smiled up at me at said, "Yes Morag, I'll watch Broocha." Safe in the knowledge that I wouldn't be too far away and that I would hear her if she wandered about I made up the feeds. I came back into the corridor to see no Jade standing at the stable door! I panicked. A stable yard has a lot of hidden dangers for young children. As I was about to rush into the yard shouting

I heard a small voice deep in conversation. I crept up to the stable door and my heart leaped into my mouth. There was Jade doing exactly what she had been told, watching Bruja. Bruja had decided to lie down while her feeds were being made. Jade had then walked into her stable and sat down on Bruja's front legs, right under her head. As I watched she was calmly taking Smarties out of her pocket and holding them for Bruja to eat, her tiny little fingers disappearing into the great mouth and Bruja gently managing to separate fingers from sweet. All the while Jade kept up a monologue conversation about this and that with Bruja who was taking everything in her stride. I tried not to let the panic show in my voice lest I startle Bruja and cause her to jump up with the inevitable effect of injuring Jade. "Hi, Jade," I said, my voice an octave or two higher than it should be. "That's Bruja's dinner ready. Out you come till I put it into her manger. Then you can sit on the wall and watch her eat." I'll never forget the look on Bruja's face as Jade got up and came out. It simply said, "It's all right, I wasn't going to hurt her." I smiled at her as she got up, "You're a good girl Bruja, a very good girl." Bruja smugly acknowledged the praise and munched away at her dinner.

Bruja was always a very nosey horse, always wanting to be in on the conversation and share all the gossip. She would sidle up to any group of humans and listen intently to what they were saying. I am sure that she filled in the rest of the herd later about what was happening in the yard. One day I was talking with some friends outside her stable and she was as usual butting into the conversation. I was drinking some tea at the time and for a laugh I asked her if she wanted a cup. She whuffed her acknowledgement, so for a joke I made her a cup with some warm water, not expecting for a moment that she would drink it, but low and behold, just so she could be one of the girls, Bruja sipped neatly on the rim of the cup as I tipped it slowly into her mouth. From that day it was a sort of ritual that if I made a cup of tea she would either have one of her own or finish off mine for me. I liked this feeling of sharing and I'm sure Bruja liked it too.

One day however she took things a bit too far. It was late August, the sky was overcast and it felt more like the start of autumn. I had been at the yard all day and was really, really hungry. One of the girls offered to go to the local chip shop and buy a pizza supper (deep fried pizza with chips, really healthy!). This went down a treat and I sat on the fence at Bruja's paddock and munched my way through the pizza. I paused for a moment to talk to my friend Karen who owned Zeus (Bruja's 'boyfriend' at the time) and didn't notice little miss nosey behind me wandering over to the fence. Bruja obviously felt that the pizza was on offer to her and neatly swiped it from my hand and stood munching my much wanted (and hardly nibbled) lunch. Karen was doubled over laughing and I couldn't help but see the funny side as I watched Bruja dispatch her unusual snack.

We stayed at Dickson's Farm for two years. I was longing again for somewhere where I could work Bruja in the winter. I had changed jobs and decided to move to a yard in Darvil. The hacking, on quiet country roads, was spectacular and there was an outdoor school for winter riding. The only drawback was the fact that the grazing was very limited. However the travelling proved to be too much for me. I would do a round trip of two hours driving to get to her and back. After only a year it was time to move again.

At this time my parents (whom I still lived with) sold up and moved to Cumbernauld. I of course followed and was surprised at the many yards available for horses in the area. I chose one with an indoor school (luxury!) and all year round grazing. Bruja loved it! We had plenty of good hacking and the opportunity to school. It was then that we started competing regularly in the local Riding Club events. Bruja was by this time sixteen years old and classed as a veteran. She did not however think like a veteran and it was always her trademark to look at least ten years younger than she was. I must have won more trophies competing at Riding Club and Unaffiliated level than I ever did as a B.S.J.A. member. Every chance we got we would hack to a local show (we never had transport, but during the summer there was always a show on at least once a week somewhere in our area). We competed in Dressage, Show Jumping, Showing, and Combined Training. Once more Bruja was in her element. She loved to perform in front of a crowd, any arguments or disagreements we may have had at home in practise were forgotten as soon as the competition started.

We competed as part of the local Riding Club's team in both Dressage and Show Jumping. When Bruja was eighteen years old I felt that the jumping side was just getting a bit much for her so I began to focus more on the Dressage. Despite her high scores and being placed every time out in the Dressage Team, Bruja was dropped because she was too old. In the same year, at the Riding Club's Annual Show, Bruja achieved probably the most rewarding prizes and one of which I am supremely proud. She not only won the Working Hunter Championship, she was placed second in the Show Hunter and swooped the Supreme Hunter Championship prize for the year.

This was also the same year that Bruja met a very

special friend. My new dog Jook. Jook was eight months old when the people who owned the yard I kept Bruja at decided they didn't want him anymore. I had known him since he was a small puppy and I said at once that I would take him. I trained him quickly to follow Bruja and trot at her heels. He learned eagerly and became a permanent attachment to Bruja and I. It was fun for Bruja to watch his antics as he scouted ahead of us. It amused her as he chased rabbits, or swam in rivers. Although she never showed any outward signs of affection for him, she definitely tolerated him and looked out for him. Jook, for his part, absolutely adored Bruja. Their favourite game was when I was loose schooling Bruja and Jook would run at her side, just in front of her, barking and challenging her to beat him. He would be daring and run flat out directly in front of her almost under her hooves. Bruja's part of the game was to look threatening and pin her ears back while snaking her head down to meet him. Occasionally she would let fly a buck and flick a hoof out to him (always impeccably judged so as not to make any contact whatsoever). I knew that it was part of the play acting on Bruja's part and that she was quite protective of Jook because if on occasion Jook would mis-time his run or not be just fast enough, Bruja would carefully adjust her stride or (as happened once or twice) have to leap over him to avoid a collision.

The mileage that Jook clocked up was phenomenal. He was with me on every ride out and during the summer months I rode out almost every day averaging five to ten mile hacks. He trotted gamely alongside Bruja as she jogged along and ran flat out as Bruja cantered. When she galloped he didn't stand a chance (not being a very large dog) but would doggedly run after us knowing that we would stop and wait if he got left too far behind. It was, I suppose, the perfect exercise for a dog. He was part of the Bruja/Morag pack and proud to be a member.

It was time to move yards yet again. Bruja I felt needed to wind down a bit and so in order to force myself not to over school her I moved to a yard with an outdoor school. The logic being that in bad weather I wouldn't be bothered to school her and would give her the day off. This didn't follow through though. Rain, hail, sleet or snow I would be out in the arena grinding round in my set exercises. I virtually never jumped Bruja now. Only little pops here and there, just to give her something different to do. This was the year that I went to America and herded cattle in Montana. It was the first time I had ridden Western and I was hooked. I came home with the goal that I would train Bruja to go Western. I had always taught her how to neck reign and so she took to the Western style like a duck to water. At nineteen years old Bruja had a new lease of life, something new to do, a new challenge.

I bought a genuine Californian Western Saddle and imported bridle and focussed on my training. Western riding is the ideal way to ride a horse. You ride the same way that you would ride for classical dressage The seat should be exactly the same. The challenge was to ask your horse to work with the same outline and shape (maybe a little less impulsion) that was expected of a novice dressage horse, but to do this with no contact on the animal's mouth and the barest whisper of an aid. In effect the horse was allowed to carry his or herself in the most natural manner. The rider was placed in the horse's centre of gravity allowing the weight to be carried effortlessly. This was exactly what Bruja needed. I would still ride mostly European to reinforce the discipline, but more and more I was beginning to use the Western way of going and it became more and more noticeable that Bruja perked up when she saw the Western saddle and sighed resignedly when she saw the European saddle.

As she started to get older Bruja realised that she just didn't have the kick power to defend herself anymore and besides, at her age she felt that she should have more decorum and respect.

A new livery client had arrived at the yard who had just bought her son a handsome black cob to learn to ride on. The cob seemed friendly enough, a little pushy but quiet for the young boy to potter around on. Bruja on the other hand had taken an instant dislike to him. She avoided any eye contact with him and seemed nervous and agitated when he was near her. When he was introduced into the field we found out why. The new horse was simply a bully. He chased the rest of the horses mercilessly, biting and kicking any that did not get out of his way. Bruja may have been old but she was more than a match for the fat black cob and easily kept herself out of range. The cob's aggression was dished out evenly around the horses and none of them liked him or stayed near him. There were more than a few kick and bite injuries during his stay at the yard and I simply couldn't understand how Bruja managed to avoid any such wounds.

One day I remember watching in disgust at how this cob behaved. The whole herd had been sleeping (except for Bruja who was on guard duty) and they were all lying down. The cob decided that it was time for him to get up, but when he got up he expected everyone else to do the same. He lunged at the nearest helpless horse who was still lying down and bit him severely on the quarters, drawing blood. He then double barrelled another horse until he got up and got out of range. This was repeated till every horse had either realised what was going on and had got up quickly or had been punished for sleeping. He then turned his attention on Bruja. He lunged at her, furious with her nonchalant attitude. Bruja calmly swished a tail at him in disgust and trotted ahead of him, just out of range of those snapping teeth. The cob was infuriated with this and broke into a fast canter (he couldn't quite manage gallop) and Bruja went into full gallop to the other end of the field and started to graze, one eye on the fast approaching cob. As soon as he was too near she flipped her tail at him and legged it to the opposite end of the field and repeated her grazing. The cob was absolutely beside himself with fury and continued after her, intent on at least giving her a bad bite. Twice across the field was almost too much for him and he was puffing really heavily by the time he reached her. She calmly flipped her tail, rolled her eye (I could almost hear her saying catch me now fat boy!) and galloped to the other side and grazed again. By now the cob was forced to trot, a heart attack threatening. He was still angry and kept at Bruja for another two laps of the field, by the time Bruja had finished with him he was standing in the middle of the field lathered in sweat and no nearer to biting her than he started out. He learned his lesson that day and never again tried to openly attack her. Bruja was too smart and fast to be caught out and when the owner finally moved the horse I'm sure the whole herd breathed a sigh of relief.

I remember one incident that happened at Summerhill and it highlighted for me the absolute trust that Bruja had in me. I was loose schooling her one dark winter night when she came diving round the corner and tried to perform an emergency stop with a spectacular spin on her back legs. Unfortunately the ground was slick and her legs slipped away from her. She twisted in the air and landed on her side with her legs trapped out through the wooden fence. She began to struggle, despite having the wind knocked out of her. I had visions of her breaking her legs on the fence when to my horror she suddenly lay still.   "That's it," I thought, "she's gone. She's broken her neck." I stood frozen for a minute numb with shock. Then I noticed her head tilting back towards me, a plaintive look of help in her eyes. I ran to her side., "Good girl, hen, whoa the girly, stay still," I mumbled to her as I approached.   I knew enough to be very careful approaching any horse that is prone on the ground. They are likely to suddenly struggle and lash out in panic. The terrible fear that any horse has about being unable to get up and run away usually takes over their minds, preventing any sensible behaviour. Bruja lay her head down and sighed in relief as I gently stroked her neck. I reviewed the situation in my mind quickly. I was alone at the yard with half a ton of horse with all four legs trapped through the fence. I couldn't risk leaving her alone to try and get help. The only thing stopping her from panicking was my presence and her total belief that no matter what happened I was going to save her. I took the gamble and did something that was very dangerous. I only acted the way I did because it was Bruja and she trusted me. I gently grabbed each front leg and pulled them back through the fence, folding them under her chin. "Good girl, whoa the girly," I constantly murmured, trying to keep fear from my voice. Bruja never moved a muscle, she knew she had to lie still and let me work. The front legs were easy. The back legs were a little harder. I got them both back through the fence, "OK hen, up, up, up, up," I said confidently. As soon as the words were out of my mouth Bruja immediately stuck her legs out to get up and instantly put them through the fence again. She was too close to the rails and had no room to manoeuvre. "Whoa, hen whoa," I said quickly and just as quickly, Bruja lay still. I repeated the exercise bringing her legs back through the fence. Then I did the impossible. I physically moved half a ton of horse over. I grabbed a back leg and pulled her onto her back. She was twisted along the middle, her front legs and head facing one way, her back legs halfway over to the other side with me hanging onto them for dear life as I tried to flip her over away from the fence. Bruja conscientiously remained still as I worked. I couldn't reach her front legs without letting go of the back legs. If I let go of the back legs she would roll back to her original position. "Come on hen, give me a hand," I said finally in exasperation as I balanced on her back legs. As soon as I asked her for her help she sprang into action, flipping over, carefully avoiding striking me, and landed on her other side. She got to her feet a little shaky but snorting with relief. I knew that I had to quickly get her confidence in herself back. I acted as though it was no big deal and picked up my lunge whip. "Come on you lazy animal, back to work." I sent her off again in a trot, scanning her carefully for any injuries or signs of lameness. After a few hesitant strides, she quickly regained her confidence and pranced about the arena like a young thing but she would never again try an emergency stop.

I started to use Bruja to help teach a girl, who had just bought a young horse, how to canter properly. The girl's position was nice and she was a quiet rider, however, when she got nervous she would grip with her legs and try to use them to hang on. Bruja decided one day that enough was enough and she was fed up having her rib cage squashed for no reason. When the girl asked for canter she started to grip, so Bruja naturally started to go faster, and faster and faster! I started to watch them helplessly as they both did the wall of death around the school. I heard myself shouting "Stop gripping with your legs" but this sound piece of logic made no sense to the poor rider who felt that this was the only thing holding her on. She must have been nearing exhaustion and had started to lose the power in her legs or perhaps she started to take my sound advice. Either way Bruja began to slow down to a canter but still refused to stop for as far as she was concerned she would keep going until the rider stopped squeezing altogether. The rider, in desperation more than anything else, took it upon herself to point Bruja at the fence at the far side of the arena. Clearly the logic being that Bruja would stop rather than run into the fence. However, a four foot six inch fence is no obstacle to a horse like Bruja and I watched in horror as I saw those powerful muscles in her quarters bunch up as she sat back on her hocks eyeing up the jump in front of her. I knew that as far as Bruja was concerned if the rider wanted to jump that was perfectly acceptable by her. I knew that this would end in tears and unable to keep the panic from my voice I shouted "DON'T POINT HER AT THE FENCE". I then witnessed one of the most amazing things I have ever seen. The rider dismounted in canter and landed neatly on her feet. Bruja, completely flabbergasted by a rider dismounting before a fence, slid to a stop and stared in utter disbelief. "Why did you jump off" I asked, open mouth and breathless. The rider looked at me solemnly and said, "I've never heard you worry about anything but when I heard the panic in your voice I realised that maybe pointing Bruja at the fence was not a very wise thing to do, so, I got off."

This was the year that I met my husband. He is my best friend and the only other living creature I have loved as much as Bruja. He understood straight away about my relationship with Bruja and Bruja took to him instantly. I taught Mark how to ride on Bruja and Bruja taught Mark how to listen and ask a horse how to work. It was a delight to be able to share Bruja with someone again. Mark, although not as dedicated as I in the winter months, helped me enormously with her. We would ride out together (me on the horse and Mark on the bike) and spent a lot of time enjoying Bruja's company and laughing at her antics. Bruja wholeheartedly approved of Mark for whom she showed deep affection.

Mark was very confident when handling Bruja and often went down the field to catch her. He normally led her up the field but on one crisp October day (after walking the full thirty acres) he thought it might be a good idea to jump on her back and walk her to the gate. Mark had been practising riding and so felt safe in the knowledge that even though he only had a head collar and a single lead rope, he could manage to guide her at a walk. Fortunately for him Bruja was wearing a New Zealand rug which gave him a little extra grip. He climbed on board and turned her face to the gate. He quietly clicked his tongue and said "on you go" never once suspecting the outcome of those fateful words.

From Bruja's point of view her reaction was perfectly reasonable. Here she was presented with a nice full thirty acres of grass and good footing. She had been training this rider how to sit on a horse for at least a year now and so decided that it was time he learned about going fast. He had after all said "on you go" and so she decided that's just what she would do, he never told her how fast she should go and so she went for top gear. Mark suddenly found himself looking at the sky as Bruja shot away with him. He scrabbled with his hands to grab some mane as his head bounced on her quarters, his legs franticly trying to hold onto the rug. He secured some mane and pulled himself forwards as he regained his balance, Bruja by this time was well on her way and moving at top speed. Mark had never forgotten the lesson that Bruja had taught him about gripping with his legs in canter (sound familiar!) and so tried to relax into the rhythm. By the time they were halfway down the field he was thoroughly enjoying himself, thrilled at the feel of those powerful muscles tearing over the ground at breakneck speed. As they neared the end of the field it quickly dawned on Mark that they were heading towards a pretty flimsy gate that was really no obstacle to Bruja. Learning to gallop was one thing, but learning to fly quite another. Mark closed his eyes and whispered "please stop Bruja, please stop Bruja, please stop….". Luckily, his prayers were answered and his fears were unfounded as Bruja bounded to an impressive stop right at the gate and stood blowing hard and immensely pleased with herself.

I remember once how Mark had the brilliant idea of filming Bruja doing one of her exciting ride outs. He cycled (on a road racing bike!) along the wooded tracks of Luggiebank where I rode and galloped Bruja. It was like making a movie. He gamely struggled through the mud on his bike, selected a likely filming spot with a good vantage of the track and would shout back to me to go. I would then gallop along the track past him, snaking through the trees at a headlong run. As soon as I was out of camera range he would shout and I would pull up, waiting for him to cycle past me to the next stretch. It was great fun and Mark was so dedicated that he even climbed a few trees to get a better shot of me running past. The result was an excellent video of Bruja racing along in her favourite past time.

I moved her once more to a yard just down the road with an indoor school. She was still with her friend Susie, a horse she had known for nearly three years and who was almost like her foal. When she had first met Susie she had mothered her to a certain extent. Bossed her when she needed bossed, bullied her when she got out of hand and showed her what it takes to be boss mare in the field.

When we arrived at the new yard I remember saying to the owner, Bruja is here until she dies. I knew that at twenty one she was too old to be continually moved on every two or three years. She had established a close relationship with Susie and both of them settled quickly into the resident herd, becoming the leaders and decision makers. Linda and I helped each other out, taking turns about doing the morning and late shift up at the yard. As Susie's confidence in the field grew she began to bully Bruja, ousting her from the top mare position. Bruja's nose was really out of joint and her confidence had taken quite a knock. For the first time in her twenty one years she was not Boss Mare and was beginning, I think, to feel her age. Susie however, soon realised that it took a lot of courage and brains to be Boss. She courted Bruja's friendship and so began a partnership that I have never seen before in horses. Susie was the brawn of the operation, her aggressive nature and flying hooves sorted out the men from the boys. Bruja on the other hand was definitely the brains. She enjoyed Susie's protection from other up and coming challengers because she knew that Susie at her core was a bit of a chicken. Susie needed Bruja's brains and courage to make the decisions for the herd. It was Bruja who decided where to graze and when etc. If another horse got out of line then it was Bruja who disciplined. If the other horse attempted to retaliate then Bruja simply called Susie in to deal with the problem. I have actually stood and watched the pair of them stand at the gate and survey the rest of the herd. Bruja would turn to Susie and make some silent comment. They would move off carefully, flanking the herd on either side. Bruja would then isolate the horse that was due to be "put in his/her place" that day and start the attack. There was no gratuitous violence. Bruja would simply bully the animal away from their chosen grazing, giving threatening looks and gestures if they didn't move quick enough. Then suddenly to the animal's surprise Susie would come charging in from the opposite direction and back up Bruja's initial threats with a more direct approach. The only horse in the field that Bruja backed down from was Susie, and the only horse that Susie would tolerate near her was Bruja.

I was now riding Bruja almost constantly in Western style and she thrived on it. I was given the chance to compete at the Scottish Western Riding Championships and was delighted to go. It was Bruja's first Western show. She romped in. We took a first, two seconds, a fourth and sixth in different classes. Not bad for a twenty two year old newcomer!

Not long after the show Linda had an accident and tore her Achilles tendon. She needed someone to ride Susie for her and keep her ticking over. There was no other rider competent enough to ride Susie (who was a bit of a handful) and so I offered to help. At this time my mother suggested that I ask Susan to come up and help. Susan was delighted. She now had an energetic three year old son Liam who loved animals and was beside himself when he was told that he could go up and visit his Auntie Morag's horsy. On Thursdays and Saturdays, Susan and Liam would go up to the yard and ride and look after Bruja. This gave me two days off a week. I sensed a feeling of finality when this happened. It was as though the circle of Bruja's life was almost complete. Here we were, almost back where we started. Susan, Bruja and me, the three amigos.

Liam loved Bruja to bits. She was so gentle with him. He would walk under her belly, his head barely above her knees. He would bravely march down the field to catch her, despite the fact that there were strange horses milling around him that must have seemed like elephants to one so small. Susan would lift him up on her back and he would "ride" Bruja up the field. Susan would often tell me how, if she was riding in the school, she would leave Liam sitting on Bruja's back outside the doors of the school and walk round the building within and open the doors.. She knew that Bruja would never do anything to hurt Liam and quite literally could be trusted to stand quietly and wait.

Bruja was very fond of Mark but she never missed an opportunity to tease him. Her timing and sense of humour was not always welcome though and one time when she gave both of us a fright. It was a cold, pitch black winter's night with a drizzle of rain just beginning. The field the herd was in was across a dark road without street lights so you could hardly see your hand in front of your face. Fortunately Bruja was usually near the gate and her distinctive white face almost glowed in the darkness.

This night however, when Mark went to catch

her (she was the last horse out) he could not see her at the gate. He shouted and shouted her name but got no response, so, fearing the worst, he set off round the field, stumbling in the darkness and mud expecting to find her stuck in a ditch or worse. He walked the whole of the field shouting her name but couldn't find her anywhere. Thinking that perhaps someone had moved the horses into another field and not told anyone he searched the next field (only 10 acres!) but still to no avail. Mark was now beginning to think someone had stolen her and so taking a deep breath he searched the first field again, this time walking the perimeter. He turned left as he entered the field and trudged through the mud around the entire edge of this dark expanse of land. As he was returning to the gate and deeply concerned he caught a glimpse of something white, just a flash, then it was gone. At this point the mud was almost knee deep, but as a peered into the night towards the hedge he had seen the white flash, there it was again. This time however he identified it as Bruja's face. "Bruja" he shouted, trying not to sound angry as he realised she had been standing there, no more than a few yards away from the gate, all along, watching him wander round the field. She had decided she was not moving from her comfortable wind break and every time he had shouted her name and looked in her direction she had turned her face away from him so he couldn't see her blaze. No doubt she thought it highly amusing to see Mark stumble in the darkness, covered in mud and filled with fear and panic, wondering what had become of her. Mark on the other hand, for quite some time, failed to see the humour of the situation!

The summer of 1997 was an eventful one for us in that it was the last time Bruja ever jumped. Susan and I rode virtually continually in Western gear. I had ridden Susie all winter for Linda who was now riding again and I felt like giving Bruja something different. I took her down the field to the outside grass arena and schooled her in her European tack. This was the first time that I felt Bruja was getting old. She found it very hard and exhausting to work properly in the dressage. I took pity on her and would have taken her straight back up the field after twenty minutes work if she hadn't shown such an interest in the small course of fences set up. I popped her over one. She loved it! After that, once a week, I would go down and pop over some small fences, building up her jumping muscles again. After about a month of this, someone suggested that I take her to a local show. I wandered down full of confidence. Mark on the other hand was not amused. He felt that it was all too much for Bruja, that she was too old and that I shouldn't be asking her to do this. I agreed with him that if she refused any fences or didn't feel right I would retire. This satisfied him and he walked down with me to the show.

We competed in the Clear Round, jumping in the small arena and, because of her age, I had only entered her into the intermediate class in the field. As I popped round the Clear Round course I really felt Bruja struggling in the deep sand arena. As usual she got a clear round and received her rosette. I watched her fondly as she arched her neck in pride at the ribbon on her bridle and stood with pride as the customary round of applause was given. As I came out of the arena the fears I had had about the intermediate class were gone. The ground in the main field was hard and much less taxing on the horses. Mark was watching me from the road. He still didn't approve of the show and wouldn't come down to the yard. I went into the class of fences not much bigger than three foot, four inches. It was then I realised how old Bruja really was. I placed her correctly at every fence because I knew she couldn't cope with any extra demands on her. I was in the same situation I had found myself in back in Bruja's B.S.J.A. days where she struggled round five to six foot courses. I was almost finished as I approached an upright set on a hill. I got the stride wrong. I put Bruja in deep expecting her to spring straight up as she did in her youth. Bruja, despite a mammoth effort on her part just didn't have the spring. She clipped the top pole as she came up. We had four faults. For the first time in her life ever, Bruja had never got through to the second round of a class. As we finished the rest of the course clear I patted and praised her on her courage and effort. People looked at me as though I was an idiot. I could see them thinking, "Why is she telling her horse it is good when it got a pole down?" "Why isn't she angry and punishing it. If that were mine I'd..." It was now that I realised how much Bruja loved me and taught me. Despite the enormous effort it must have taken for her to go round the course, I had sensed the annoyance and disappointment in her for taking down a pole. I did what was right, I thanked her for her brave effort and told her that it didn't matter; she was still the best horse in the world as far as I was concerned.

I rode out of the yard knowing that I would never compete Bruja in jumping again and I was not unhappy. Mark met me at the corner, a knowing look in his eye. "You were right honey," I said, "She's too old now."

The summer rolled on and Susan and I went down the field one day to give Bruja a little jump for fun. Susan had not jumped Bruja since those early days when I had broken my collar bone. I warmed Bruja up and popped her over a small double. Susan put the fence up for me and I finished at around three feet. Susan got on and I put the fence down for her. I watched Bruja carefully for any signs of stress or tiredness, but she was in her element. I had carefully strode the fence to suit her perfectly. The opening fence was a two foot cross bar with one stride onto a nice upright. A simple fence for her and placed so that she would never be wrong. As Susan continued to jump her, I would put up the upright until, as I shouted, "Last time over this one," the pole was just about four foot high. Bruja came in with her usual gusto, a look of smug pleasure on her face as she spotted the fence. She knew she could do it and she wanted to do it for Susan. She wanted Susan to feel the same exhilaration that I had felt for many years as she flew over the fence. We had collected an audience of other livery clients, who were trying very hard not to make it look obvious that they were watching. Bruja bounded into the double and flew over the upright, clearing it by at least six inches. She was in her element. Susan let out a whoop of pleasure and surprise as she felt the power and confidence well up from Bruja. I saw Bruja's face and knew that she had given her all for that one last jump. "That'll do her," I said to Susan's smiling face, "She's had enough." Susan agreed, gasping in delight at the exhilaration of jumping a bold and brave horse. It was the last time Bruja ever jumped.

I never rode Bruja in her European tack again. We concentrated only on Western. I knew she was getting old and she could only give her best in the Western tack. Our days were taken up with hacking out and having fun. Just like the old days. In October of 1997 I was offered the use of a trailer and car to tow it in order to compete at a Western show. It was a great day out for Susan and me. We felt proud as punch as we drove along with our horse in the back, looking smart and feeling good. We arrived at the show and began our classes. Susan did three and I did three. Once again Bruja excelled herself, trying her hardest and winning three rosettes. Susan's Mum and Dad met us at the show and of course Liam was there as well. Everyone watched in silent awe as this tiny four year old was put up onto Bruja's back. "Right Liam," I said, "you're my groom, so you know what that means don't you?" "Yes Auntie Morag," said Liam, "I've got to warm up Bruja for you." His little legs struck Bruja's saddle as he said in a commanding voice, "Walk on Bruja!" Bruja threw me a quick glance to make sure that it was OK for her to move. I gave her a smile and a nod and off she went with this tiny rider, looking more like a pea on a mountain than anything else. It was a brilliant day, it was a perfect day and it was Bruja's last show.

It must have been a few weeks after the show that Mark and I were up one Friday night. I was preparing her stable for her and Mark went out to catch her. I tidied her bed, made up her night and morning feeds and filled her hay manger. I strolled about wondering what was taking Mark so long. Eventually I went over to the field gate to see where they were. There was Mark, not too far from the gate standing by Bruja's side and patting her. He saw me and suddenly started waving frantically for me to come down. My heart leaped into my mouth. Something must be very wrong.

I walked quickly down the field trying not to run and trying not to panic. I studied Bruja as I approached them. I noticed Bruja holding her left front leg off the ground. She was resting the toe slightly on the ground, but refused to put any weight on it. I could see she was breathing heavily and sweat was starting to appear on her flanks. "This is it," I thought, "She's broken her leg. I'll have to have her shot!" I looked at her face with her frightened eyes. Mark was really worried. "I didn't want to move her. She can't put any weight on her leg." "It's OK my darling," I said, "You did the right thing." I began to examine her leg carefully. She allowed me to manipulate her joints and flex her leg at the knee and elbow. I stood up puzzled. I couldn't feel any obvious breaks. What was wrong? "We'll need to get her up the field. You go on one side, I'll go on the other. As she hops, try and support her weight. We'll take it one step at a time." Slowly, inch by inch, we crawled up the field. Bruja relied heavily on Mark and I, leaning on us as she gamely tried to move towards the gate. She knew what we wanted; she knew that she needed to be in her stable and she knew that we were going to try to make her better.

When she finally made it to her box she was gasping for breath and sweating hard. I hosed her legs down, feeling for any signs of heat. Putting her sweat rug on her I put her in her box and put support bandages on all of her legs. I couldn't find anything obvious and so opted for the most likely cause. "She may have an abscess in her foot. I'll call Mr Jarvie tonight and ask him to come out tomorrow morning to dig it out." By the time we left Bruja was putting her foot flat on the ground and seemed to be a lot more relaxed.

I called Susan that night and explained that Bruja couldn't be ridden as I thought she had an abscess. Susan said she would bring Liam up to see her anyway. Saturday morning came and I went up to see Bruja and wait for the Blacksmith. Bruja had recovered remarkably in the short time. She was using her leg again, albeit a bit stiffly and cautiously. I lead her out and un-bandaged her legs, hosing them just for good measure. I put her back into her box and re-bandaged her. Then settled down to wait. It wasn't long before Bruja lay down for a sleep. I opened her door and went in and sat with her. Jook came in as well and curled up in a corner. Bruja as usual lay flat out and snored. Susan and Liam appeared and I motioned for them to come in quietly. Susan had seen Bruja sleeping before but it was a new experience for Liam and his face was a picture as he came and sat in the box with us. Susan explained that it was OK and that Bruja was just resting her sore toe. We all sat together in her bed, listening to her snore, feeling honoured that we were all so trusted by Bruja. Mr Jarvie arrived not long after Bruja awoke and stood. He examined her foot then her legs then asked to see her out. By this time she was walking normally and I myself thought it very strange. "I can't see anything in her foot at all." said Mr Jarvie, "Is she better than last night?" "Much, she couldn't put any weight on it at all." He started to examine her shoulder and move her neck up and down, "The only thing I can think it may have been is a trapped nerve or knock she's got on her shoulder. Maybe she went down and rolled on a stone awkwardly or cricked her neck. Horses are funny about pain. There's a possibility she hurt herself and got scared to put her foot down." I nodded in agreement. We decided to put her back out in the field and keep an eye on her. This we did and Bruja was fully recovered in a few days. The wisdom of Mr Jarvie was proved right once more.

The winter set in and life resumed its usual routine. In January 1998 I sold my European saddle. It hadn't been used in six months and I knew that it wasn't right to waste a perfectly good piece of tack. Let someone else get use of it and hopefully have as much fun as I had had. I began to teach on and off a young girl called Semera. She had learned to ride the previous Summer on Bruja and roughly once a week would come along for a half hour lesson. She was a very good rider and Bruja responded well to her, knowing that it was an easy half hour if it was a beginner lesson. There was a break of about a month when Semera couldn't get up to ride Bruja and I began to give her some extra days off. I sensed a depression in Bruja that I had never sensed before. In February Mark and I went to Ireland for a weekend break. Linda and Susan looked after Bruja for me. On my return Susan voiced her concern for Bruja, "She's just not eating like she used to." I tried to coax her to eat her feed, but she just seemed so tired all of the time.

On Monday 30 March 1998 I rode Bruja for the very last time. I had taken the day off work and had come up to the yard early afternoon. I brought her in and spent time grooming her and generally making a fuss of her. I brought out my Western tack and she nosed it sighing. I had noticed that recently when she came in she would search the door for the saddle. If there was no saddle then she brightened up knowing she would have no work. I tacked her up and planned my route. I was running out of light so I chose a shorter trip that took jus thirty minutes and gave us the opportunity to sneak into a field for a quick gallop. I set off up the hill and was immediately alerted to something odd about Bruja. I just couldn't feel her legs.

She had always seemed so strong and sure, now I felt as though her legs were numb and shaky, as though they could give at any moment. I looked at her brave face and she gamely held her head arched and jogged up the steep hill. At the top she was puffing for breath but, recognising the route I was taking and itching for a gallop, she stepped out and carried on. I sat still and asked for nothing. I let her do what she wanted, how she wanted. We walked down the hill towards the field. I felt her jog on as she approached the gate, willing to take me in and go for a run. A voice in my head said, "Don't do it!" I gently pulled her up and turned her around. "It's OK hen, we'll gallop another day." As we went back to the yard I put her on a grass verge and let her canter. I let her choose her pace and felt her try to run, but no power was in those great muscles. Her strong sure legs were failing her. I pulled her up and walked her home, making much of her and grooming her gently before I gave her her feed. She walked into her box and tried to eat. She munched slowly for about five minutes then left her feed and nosed her hay. I left with a sense of foreboding.

On the Tuesday it was her day off. Linda looked after her, bringing her in and feeding her. On the Wednesday Semera came up for her usual lesson. I brought Bruja in from the field and took off her rugs. I gasped in shock at what I saw. Semera, who hadn't seen Bruja for a month exclaimed in surprise. This powerful friend was fading. The strong muscles of her quarters were wasting away. I ran my hand over her ribs and felt the flesh thin, barely disguising the bones. "Morag, Bruja looks very tired today," said Semera tactfully. I patted Bruja's neck and looked at her willing eyes. "Let's take her out for a short time and see how she is," I said. We tacked her up and took her into the arena. Bruja as ever was delighted to be ridden. She trotted around the arena as Semera asked her to work. I couldn't speak. Bruja was just shy of twenty four years old and she looked her age for the first time in her life. I saw the wasted muscles of her quarters, the thinness of her neck and the deep sunken eyes. After about ten minutes Semera said, "I think we should stop now, I think Bruja is too tired today." "Yes, I think you're right Semera," I whispered. We took her back to the yard and I called Linda over. "Look at this," I said. Linda's expression said it all. She was as experienced as me and could recognise as I could that this was serious. Bruja was fading fast. We put her into her bed and again she wouldn't eat her feed. I took Semera home and only when she had left the car did I break down in tears. I knew that this profound moment in my life was racing to a close.

Thursday I put her out by herself in what we called the starvation paddock. It was a very small field that was usually short of grass. However, because it had been empty all summer and winter it was lusher than the main grazing fields. I hoped against hope that if I could only get her to eat that she would recover her strength. I left her extra hay and feeding as I walked away. That night I brought her in I couldn't see any difference in her weight. That was encouraging; at least she wasn't getting thinner. On Friday I put her out in the paddock again. That night I was up a little later than expected and Linda had already brought her in and rugged and fed her. She looked so contented munching her hay that I didn't have the heart to disturb her.

Susan was supposed to be coming up on Saturday 4 April 1998 to ride her so I went up early to make sure she was OK. I mucked her out and took off her rugs to put on her outdoor New Zealand. As the rugs came off I dropped them to the floor, a moan of agony escaping my lips. My poor beautiful Bruja was fading to a skeleton. Her body weight must have halved in these few short days. I had already checked her feed manger and noted that her evening feed had not been touched. She hadn't drunk any water and her hay was barely disturbed. Her tail was clean of shavings so she hadn't laid down that night at all. Her legs were swollen from standing all night. "It's OK my baby girl, its OK." I patted her neck and she watched me with dull and sad eyes. I put her stable rug back on and went home knowing that now I had to be strong for her, for my friend.

The Parting II

I blinked the tears from my eyes as I picked up the phone to call Susan. She sounded surprised when I called, "Susan, It's Morag, Bruja's not well, the vet is coming up. Don't bring Liam but get out here fast."
"OK," was the quiet response.

As soon as Susan arrived we went back up to the yard to wait. I had called my Mum and Dad and asked them to be there. I had called Linda and asked her to come quickly. As Mark, Susan, Mum and Dad and I stood in her stable waiting for the vet it was the hardest thing in the world for me to do to keep calm. I didn't want to cry, I didn't want to upset Bruja. She mustn't suspect anything. I was stupid to think Bruja didn't know what was going on. She was affectionate with everyone, giving them each a private moment of comfort, a private goodbye. The vet arrived. I had stressed to her that although she didn't know Bruja, she should try to visualise a muscular fit big horse so that when she saw the beast standing in the box she would realise how much weight had been lost. I don't even know her name, but her compassion and sensitivity was what helped me cope. She examined Bruja carefully and thoroughly. She suspected as I did that Bruja had liver failure, a common complaint in old horses. She knew as I did that by the time any blood tests came back from the lab the horse would be dead. She finally spoke, "She has a very bad heart murmur, her circulation is bad and her lungs are filling with fluid, that's why she won't lie down. It is not treatable and will not get better." She looked me straight in the eye as she said this. It was my decision. It surprised me how easy it was to say those fateful words, "Do it now." This was my friend, my soul mate and she was in pain and suffering. Every time Bruja had been in pain in her life she knew it would be me who would take the pain away. She knew I would help her.

We led her quietly round to the indoor school and closed the door. Bruja stood still as we took off the head collar and I held her with a rope round her neck. As the injection went in I talked to her all the time, "Where's my little baby girl? Aw the girly, aw the baby girls tired, aw shush the baby girl, good girl Bruja, good girl." I didn't cry. I didn't sound upset. I wouldn't do it. I wanted my voice, telling her how good she was, to be the last thing she heard. As the injection took effect she staggered. "Let her go," said the vet. I let the rope slip away from her neck as she went down, a mild look of surprise on her face. Usually when they go down a horse will struggle in panic. As soon as she hit the ground I ran to her side. "Be careful," the vet started to say, expecting Bruja to struggle. But I wouldn't let my friend panic. I wouldn't let her last moments be filled with fear and confusion. As soon as my hand touched her neck she looked at me with blurry eyes. "It's OK my baby girl, it OK. Lie still hen, good girly." I felt her relax; I felt the fight leave her as she gratefully gave in to the anaesthetic. I watched my friend die. I talked to her constantly till I saw her magnificent spirit of fire leave her eyes. I waited till the end before I expressed my grief. I heard the vet say, "That's her gone," before I let go. I remember standing up and turning away, I dropped the rope and wailed a soul piercing scream as I felt her leave this world and felt strong arms around me as Mark held me close, trying to take the pain I felt away.

After a few minutes I regained control. There were still things for me to do. I thanked the vet who had stayed with us. She tried to say the right things. I could see that she too was upset by what she had seen. "It was a brave thing you did," she said, "It was the right thing you did." I knew she was right but I still felt awful. Mark, Susan and I all stayed until the Knacker man came. Susan and Mark had never seen this before, but I had. I always stayed with a horse until the Knackerer had taken them onto the lorry. It was my way of confirming to myself that they had really gone, that all that was left was the shell. Mark had visions of some dreadful accident happening, like Bruja's head being ripped off as she was dragged onto the lorry. I made myself watch and I am glad I did. I had seen my friend die and now watched as her shell was taken away to be burned. The Knackerer worked quickly and was as sensitive as he could be. I watched the lorry go then turned to go back into the yard. Linda hadn't made it on time. She drove up a mere five minutes later. "She's gone," I said as Linda looked uncomprehendingly at Mark then Susan and me. "That's her away." Linda broke down in tears, "I didn't know it was that bad, I didn't get here on time." "It's OK hen," I said, "It was her heart."

A New Beginning

This is Bruja's story. I wanted to write it, I wanted to share all of her wonderful life with as many people as possible. Bruja touched all who knew her, but no one knows the full story. This is it. This is something I have had to do. Many tears have been shed as I have written this account; many heartaches have been felt as I recall that incredible oneness I had with my friend. I will never forget her. A piece of me died with Bruja that day, but it is only now that I can fully understand the lessons that she has taught me. It is only now that I wish to carry on her teachings with another horse.

I recently watched the film Black Beauty and remember the part where Beauty is to be sold after being a cab horse. "Sold," says Beauty, "That is a word every horse knows and dreads." I pride myself with the knowledge that Bruja only heard that word twice in her life. Once when Billy Stewart bought her and once when she passed to me. I was the one constant in her life. I was honoured to be her friend.

In those final days I often wished that I would

simply go to the yard one day and just find her gone. I dreaded having to be the one who made the decision to put her down. But now that I have done the deed I can honestly say that I am glad that she did not die alone. She was surrounded by the people who loved her most in the world and the last face she saw was mine. The last words she heard was me telling her she was a "good girl". This was right. This was how it was meant to be.

I would be a liar to say that I don't miss her terribly. Sometimes the pain is so great it is like a knife in my heart. The tears I shed are tears of longing. The emptiness I feel is slowly healing, but the hurt goes on. I kept most of her rugs and her western saddle. Sometimes I go out into the shed and just stand and smell her rugs, her saddlecloth, her saddle. The memories of her come flooding back and all are happy and filled with excitement. We had a good time. We had a good life and I am glad that Bruja is no longer in pain and if there is a heaven for all living things that she will be there as she was, young and vibrant once more.

I have applied to the ILPH (International League for the Protection of Horses) to adopt a horse. One day the story will continue. One day Bruja's heart and spirit will touch others again.

The Story Continues

A few months after Bruja had died, a friend called and offered me the chance to purchase her one-year-old filly. I went up to see the horse, but, I was still very raw inside and the price she wanted was more than I could afford.

At the same yard, the day before , a yearling colt had just arrived. He stood in a stable next to his mother, a look of real attitude about him. I glanced through the doorway at this arrogant piece of work. A yellow gold coat gleamed in the sunlight, the splashes of white markings on his body complementing his four white legs and white face. I remember thinking that this little chap would be a really handsome little sprog one day. I knew the girl who owned him and I knew she would never sell him. Inside I was perhaps a little jealous, but at the same time glad for the horse because he couldn't have asked for a better owner than he had found in Leslie.

A year later, in March 1999, I went back up to my friend's yard to pick up some of Bruja's old rugs that she had been storing for me. I don't know why *I* did this, the rugs had been lying for a year and I had given them no more thought. I didn't need the rugs for anything; there was just an incessant nagging in my mind that I must go up to Sarah's yard. Sarah showed me her latest foal, a six-month-old Appaloosa and his extremely nervous mother. I admired the colt and glanced again at the stable next door. A handsome liver chestnut with a white blaze stared at me over the door. "Is this Paddy?" I asked. Sarah said yes. I looked over the door at the most strikingly handsome horse I had seen in a long time. He had filled out and since he had been gelded his entire attitude had been turned to intelligence and good humour. "What is Leslie doing with him now?" It was then that the bombshell struck. Sarah told me that Leslie had hit on some hard times and would have to sell Paddy. He had been advertised in Horse & Pony Magazine just this week. I was gob smacked by the coincidence. The advert would have appeared in the Horse & Pony Magazine that very weekend. He would be snapped up. I asked Sarah how much Leslie was looking for him. She said she would find out and let me know.

Later that night Leslie called me at home. "Morag, Sarah tells me you are interested in Paddy?" "Yes that's right," I replied. "Well Morag," continued Leslie, "you have no idea how glad I am that it is you who wants to buy him. He couldn't go to a better home. I'm looking for £800." My heart leaped. He was more than worth the money. The trouble was I didn't have it at present and wouldn't have it till at least July. I told Leslie this and waited for her response. "Morag," she said, "You can take him just now and give me the money when you want. I want Paddy to go to someone who will love him and look after him. I know how good you were to Bruja, I know how good a horse she was and I want Paddy to have the same chance to shine like Bruja did." For some time neither of us could speak as we both had a little cry in memory of the wee black mare.

Mark bought Paddy for me. I couldn't believe my luck. Paddy arrived in Bruja's old stable at the last yard she had been on exactly a year and one week after her death. This handsome two-year-old beamed out over the door, a startling resemblance to Bruja in mannerisms and quiet good humour.

We had decided that our next horse should be called Brogan. I do not like to change a horse's name, but Paddy became Brogan and uses the full Sunday name of Paddy Brogan on special occasions.

I made a solemn promise to Bruja the day he arrived. I would remember the mistakes I had made with her, I would never forget what she had taught me. I would try very hard to listen to Brogan and to understand how he thought and felt. He would not experience the confusion and upset that Bruja no doubt felt in her early years. He would continue the legacy that Bruja had given me.

If ever I feel myself becoming impatient or exasperated, I hear Bruja say to me, "No," "remember what I have shown you, do as I have asked."

One day I will sit tall on Brogan's back and feel the oneness again. On this day I will thank Bruja for all that she has done and continues to do.

No Regrets

A last twitch from that knowing ear, slowly I watch her fire disappear.

Our souls join together one last time then the spark is gone.

And still her spirit lives on, burning in the hearts of the ones with whom she shared her gift.

They only need to close their eyes and remember, to feel that power, the rush, in this she will never go.

Bruja was and still is unique but don't we all feel this way about the things that touch our very core.

Bruja had character, strength, spirit and a willingness to teach us how to live.

I only felt this a few times, the oneness.

I know that I will feel that fire again.

Bruja tried to teach me so much and I feel that I learned so little from her; one thing I do know is that I'll never try to teach a horse how to be a horse.

NO REGRETS, we all make mistakes, it's the way we learn, it's the way we live.

I do miss that auld bag, funny eh?

Mark Higgins

Lightning Source UK Ltd.
Milton Keynes UK
UKOW041837150413

209269UK00001B/71/P